How to **organize** your
scrapbook
workspace
storage solutions for any budget

**MEMORY
MAKERS
BOOKS**

Executive Editor Kerry Arquette   Founder Michele Gerbrandt

Senior Editor MaryJo Regier

Art Director Andrea Zocchi

Designer Nick Nyffeler

Art Acquisitions Editor Janetta Wieneke

Craft Editor Jodi Amidei

Photographer Ken Trujillo

Contributing Photographers Christina Dooley, Jim Gregg, Brenda Martinez, Jennifer Reeves

Contributing Writers Kathleen Aho, Maureen Behnke, Darlene D'Agostino, Stacey Gustafson, Julie Labuszewski,
Heath McKenny, Lori Elkins Solomon

Contributing Artists Jodi Amidei, Kari Hansen-Daffin, Emily Curry Hitchingham, Torrey Miller, MaryJo Regier, Janetta Wieneke

Set Construction Marc Creedon, Jim Gregg, Bill Kreil, Brittany Mahrer

Editorial Support Emily Curry Hitchingham, Debbie Mock, Dena Twinem

Hand Model Emily Curry Hitchingham

Published by Memory Makers Books, an imprint of F & W Publications, Inc.
12365 Huron Street, Suite 500, Denver, CO 80234
Phone 1-800-254-9124
First edition. Printed in Singapore.
07 06 05 04 03 5 4 3 2 1

Library of Congress Cataloging-in-Publication Data

How to organize your scrapbook workspace : storage solutions for any budget
    p. cm.
Includes bibliographical references and index.
ISBN 1-892127-18-0
1. Storage in the home. 2. Scrapbooks--Equipment and supplies. 3. Photograph
albums--Equipment and supplies. I. Memory Makers Books.

TX309.H685 2003
648'.8--dc22

2003065188

Distributed to trade and art markets by
F & W Publications, Inc.
4700 East Galbraith Road, Cincinnati, OH 45236
Phone 1-800-289-0963

ISBN 1-892127-18-0
Memory Makers Books is the home of *Memory Makers*, the scrapbook magazine dedicated to
educating and inspiring scrapbookers. To subscribe, or for more information, call 1-800-366-6465.
Visit us on the Internet at www.memorymakersmagazine.com

This book belongs to

_____

We dedicate this book to all of our _Memory Makers_ contributors
who shared their winning organizational ideas and tips and to dedicated scrapbookers
everywhere who are determined to find more time for the passionate hobby of scrapbooking!
We extend a heartfelt "thank you" to the many product manufacturers featured
herein for their generous contributions to this project.

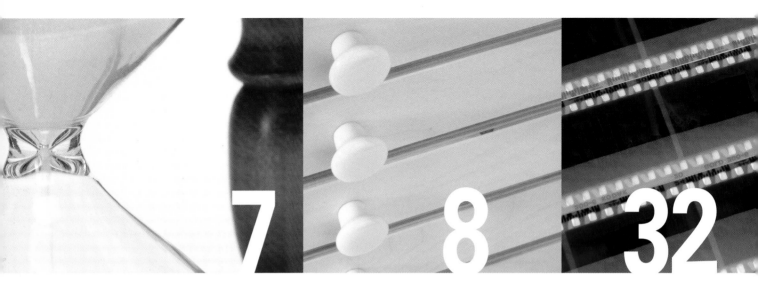

TABLE OF CONTENTS

Introduction

The hobby of scrapbooking brings with it an immense amount of tools and supplies, with appealing new stuff appearing in the stores almost daily. And regardless of how we currently store our scrapbook "stuff," we always feel the need to be better organized. Like me, perhaps you need better scrapbook organization or workspace planning solutions. Maybe your photos and negatives are in such disarray that it's hard to settle on the next scrapbook page to make. Or maybe your papers, stickers and embellishments are stacked on every horizontal surface and the clutter overcomes your urge to crop. If you have the desire to get organized "someday," realize that someday never arrives without a commitment to take those first steps at getting organized. Take the initiative and start your organizational project today!

This book is designed so that you can set your own pace. You can either work through it in front-to-back fashion to organize absolutely everything you own or you can pick and choose which areas or items need work the most. You will learn how to create a plan of action, take stock of your available space options, plan for small spaces and plan storage that is right for you, undertake budget considerations, create a personalized floor plan, organize your scrapbook tools and supplies, efficiently plan page kits and discover solutions for streamlined and effective cropping on the go. Further, we explore countless storage products and containers from product manufacturers who are as dedicated as we are to helping you get and stay organized.

In addition to the pull-up-your-shirt-sleeves, nuts-and-bolts organizational know-how, we've included some really fun and unique ideas, too. I think you will love our section on room colors for enhanced creativity, ideas for the ergonomic workspace, how to host a swap, frugal flea-market finds, antiques in the workspace and storage that can be found around the house. You'll find one of the most revealing ideas in our section on trading scrapbook workspaces. Once they thought their workspaces were organized, we challenged two scrapbookers to trade workspaces for a day and create a page. Both women came away with organizational ideas that they have since implemented for their own workspaces as well as advice for one another on things they could do differently to streamline efficiency. It's an idea that you may enjoy doing with one of your own scrapbook buddies; it's quite a telling and rewarding experience!

Start at the beginning of this book or wherever you need the most help. It is all up to you. Take a look through the Table of Contents as an overview of what is available. Once you work through all the chapters of this book, you will definitely be a more organized and efficient scrapbooker! Whether you have a small nook or a large studio, these tips will help you get your scrapbooking act together. Working toward your goals for as little as ten to fifteen minutes a day will yield fantastic changes over time. Every scrapbooker wants to feel organized and productive as she creates a legacy for her family. This book is a tool that will help you become more productive and keep your workspace clutter-free.

Michele

Michele Gerbrandt
Founding Editor
Memory Makers magazine

Finding Time to Get Organized

The late, great singer Jim Croce hit the nail on the head: "There never seems to be enough time, to do the things you want to do, once you find them." A counterproductive—albeit far-too-true—lament in today's busy lifestyles where spare time is a commodity. However, by purchasing this book, you made a conscious decision to overcome the obstacles of clutter and chaos in an effort to be more productive. Ironically, in order to get organized, you have to find time in your busy schedule to commit to the process of getting organized. Squeeze more time out of every day with the following ideas.

ANALYZE HOW YOU SPEND TIME

Keep a time log for a week to identify vacant blocks of time or look back at a monthly calendar to determine the best time to get organized. Early birds may prefer rising thirty minutes earlier each morning whereas night owls tend to work best later in the evening. When are you willing to devote time to getting organized?

Once you have defined the best time to work, identify how you or others may be wasting your precious time and try to avoid those time wasters during your organizational phase. Typical time wasters include misuse of, or straying on, computer time, lengthy phone calls, inability to say "no" to people, frequently allowing interruptions, reading junk mail and watching too much television. In addition to avoiding time-wasting traps, perhaps hire someone else to do light housekeeping, baby-sitting, even laundry. Don't try to do it all. Use every available resource to squeeze spare moments from each day.

WAYS TO FIND TIME

According to Joe Peraino, Ph.D., in *Improving Productivity by Getting Organized*, "One minute of planning saves five minutes of execution." These methods will enable you to be five times more productive:

SET SIMPLE, OBTAINABLE GOALS

Start by setting realistic goals for yourself and determine how often you can devote time to getting organized. Are you realistically able to spend time once a day, week, or month? Make a deadline such as, "Within three months, my workspace will be organized." Make time for getting organized—and later remaining organized—a regular habit.

BEGIN BY PICKING A PROJECT

Looking at "the big picture" can be overwhelming. Select one project with which to begin. Your choices may include setting up your workspace with furniture, lighting and the essentials; sorting years of photos and negatives; or organizing non-consumable or consumable tools and supplies.

BREAK THE PROJECT INTO SMALLER PIECES

Even though you probably understand that the big picture includes organizing your entire scrapbook workspace, this book will help you achieve success by breaking the task into smaller, more manageable chunks. Isolate one area in which to begin. Collect everything in a large, open space where you can leave things out undisturbed for a couple days, if necessary.

ATTACK AND HAVE FUN

The good news is that this process can be fun once you begin to see the advantages of getting organized. Get the most out of your time by eliminating distractions. Turn off the phone. Organize in a quiet place out of the main runway of the home. By investing time, you will actually be able to gain time to scrapbook. One thing that you cannot recycle is wasted time, so get started today!

Finding time to get organized involves making a commitment to the task at hand. Use a calendar to plot out a general time-frame in which to get fully organized—even if it's just 30 minutes each day—and try hard to stick to it. Before you know it, you'll have more time for scrapbooking!

CREATING A PLAN OF ACTION

Every scrapbooker needs a place, even if it is a small one, to work on her scrapbooks at home. This highly rewarding hobby brings with it a lot of tools and supplies. Enough so that when they are unorganized and in disarray, it takes the fun out of the hobby. For a brief time, let us ignore the supplies and truly analyze the workspace itself. Start by taking stock of the physical space, furniture, shelving and lighting and if what you have is or is not working for you. Take notes as you work through the sections of this book. This will help you focus on the personalized needs of your workspace.

Scrapbook spaces can range from a scrapbook tote in the closet all the way up to a large artist-style studio with all the perks. Surprisingly, the mark of a productive scrapbook area is not purely a size consideration. Organization and efficiency are more important than square footage. Most scrapbookers have to carve out a space in their homes to call their own.

In this chapter, you'll learn how to start with an honest assessment of your space needs and continue working through every problem area in your scrapbook workspace. You will soon be well on your way to a functional workspace solution. Keep in mind that you want to start by changing small, but definite areas of your workspace. Whether you need to create a new space, declutter and consolidate the current one, or just rearrange the work area, the key is to do a little at a time.

Organization is more than just cleaning up again and again or putting things out of sight. It is creating a system that works for you in the long term. It takes time to create an effective workspace, but it is worthwhile. Tackle a section of your space or a chapter of this book at a time. Make informed decisions. Even if you are in chaos now, soon you will have a plan for your space and all your tools and supplies that suits your budget and the way in which you work.

Are You Ready for Change?

Something has got to give! New scrapbook supplies find their way home in bags that get piled behind doors. Papers are here and scissors are there. Adhesive cartridges are empty and in need of refilling. Inspirations, torn from magazines, overflow from their designated spot in an absolute symphony of disarray. And don't even look in the sticker box or the embellishments drawer! Unorganized scrapbook supplies can be overwhelming. You simply can't scrapbook when you spend all of your time pawing through bins, drawers and bags looking for stuff. If you're reading this book, and if your scrapbook workspace looks even remotely like the one shown below, you have obviously reached the point where you are ready for change.

Well-stocked chaos is the hallmark of an extremely busy scrapbook artist, as witnessed in this photo of Torrey Miller's (Thornton, Colorado; 2003 Memory Makers Master) scrapbook workspace. Even if you feel organized, there is always room for improvement. Assessing when and how you scrapbook—or rather, would like to scrapbook—can provide useful insights into effective changes that need to be made in your scrapbook workspace. For the record, Torrey's workspace has since been restored to its highly organized and efficient splendor.

Where to Start

What is driving you most crazy? What changes would you like to make in your scrapbook work-space? Start by taking stock of the problem. Get out a pen and paper and make a "problems" list. Dream a little. Is your work surface too small? Does your back ache after sitting in your chair for an hour? Do you have enough drawer space? Enough adequate storage units? Have you made the best use of your existing floor and wall space? Does the arrangement of your furnishings coincide with the way you work? Are you tired of feeling cramped? Is that cupboard door with a loose handle bugging you? Write it down! Order the problems from the most annoying to the least annoying, and tackle the most problematic areas first.

HOW DO YOU SCRAPBOOK?

What is the sequential order in which you create a scrapbook page? Do you work very methodically, taking lots of time to concept your pages and gather the appropriate materials before you begin? Do you skip the page concepting altogether and jump right in to page design, drawing materials from here and there on the fly? Do you work from right to left or left to right? Do you spend a lot of time switching from sitting to standing? Or moving your chair from side to side or forward and backward in order to gather scrapbook materials? Do you find that you go out into the living room to match papers to photos because the lighting is better there? Do you brush scraps to the floor and vacuum or sweep later or do you brush stuff into a trash bin as you go along? Recognize that even the tiniest of changes to your workspace may greatly enhance the time you get to spend on scrapbooking!

WHEN DO YOU SCRAPBOOK?

When do you tend to scrapbook the most? If you can't seem to find the time, ask yourself when you might best fit it in. Are you a loner who gets things done in the middle of the night? Or are you a busy mom who needs her sleep? Do you work outside the home and view your space as a refuge? Do you scrapbook only at crops or do you scrapbook in random 30-minute sessions at home? Do you like the whirl of activity in the family room? Or do you need a weekly "silent hour" or two alone to work? If you hate being alone, a large solitary studio will not be a fun place for you. If you can't think when the television is on, a workspace in the family room may be a bad choice. *When* you scrapbook will give you the largest clue to *where* you should scrapbook.

Rewards

If you feel intimidated by the task ahead of you, plan to reward yourself in small ways for the progress you will be making. Refrain from shopping for or buying any new scrapbook tools and supplies at this point; you'll only compound the matter of chaos. Instead, make a list of ten weeks of "treats" that you would like as small rewards, one after each week of dedicated organizational work. Here are a few ideas:

- Light some scented candles for ambiance
- Take a well-deserved nap
- Rent a movie you've been longing to see
- Take someone special out for dessert
- Purchase that awesome set of earrings or shoes you've had your eyes on
- Take a leisurely walk with an old friend

- Call someone special long distance
- Get a soothing manicure; you may need it
- Load your CD player with your favorite recording artists and blare the music until everyone runs from the house
- Take a long, steamy bubble bath
- Go to bed two hours early, shut and lock the door, and read something really good

Sizing Up Your Workspace Options

Take stock of what you currently have available for workspace. Are you happy with it? If you are truly happy, you can probably skip to chapter 2. If not, examine your home for a nook or area where you might work happily. Think about your personal preferences. Ask yourself if you prefer to be in the room with the action or do you just want peace and a little music to help you create? Be practical! Many scrapbookers with large designated scrapbook rooms have found they miss the interaction with the family in the family room. Choose a space that will fit your hobby goals and your personal needs. Bring all of your scrapbook supplies into that area and keep them close to your work table. Being able to retrieve your items in seconds will speed the creation of your pages. You do not want to have to walk to another room for each item you use in this "getting organized" phase or when scrapbooking.

WHERE CAN I SQUEEZE IN A SCRAPBOOK AREA?

Look at all the rooms in your home. How are they being used? Is there a room that was originally designated for one activity but is no longer needed in that capacity? Formal dining rooms, lofts, billiard/pool rooms, dens, libraries, extra bedrooms, three-season porches, home gyms, "catch-all" rooms and base-ments are often underutilized spaces. Belongings and junk stored in these rooms can be moved elsewhere to create a few feet of space for your scrapbook area. Forget what the builders designed a room to be—make it what you need it to be!

WHAT KIND OF STORAGE WILL A NEW AREA REQUIRE?

Once you have selected a potential spot, look at the area as a professional organizer would. Do you have room for a full-fledged desk? Do you have room only to tuck in a folding card table or drop-down, hinged shelf-desk? Furnishings should be comfortable and inviting as well as functional. If a chair is too stiff to sit in for long periods of time, it is inappropriate for scrapbooking. A desk or plain pine door sitting atop two unfinished night stands can function well as a workspace if it is the right height for you. There should be a balance of actual desktop workspace and storage space. Too much of one without the other will leave you frustrated and unproductive.

Examine under-utilized areas of your home for potential spots to carve out a scrapbook workspace. MaryJo Regier (Memory Makers Senior Book Editor) considered convert-ing a three-season porch to a workspace, but Colorado's winter cold dissuaded her. Her second and final option was to get rid of two older computers on an upstairs loft and claim it for scrapbooking. The loft is a shared space (see page 16) and a pathway between bedrooms; furniture that closes up to conceal its contents was an important factor. The ability to see over the railing to the front door, two different family rooms and the entire upstairs from the loft was also important for this busy mom of four.

Planning for Small Spaces

With scrapbooking, it's not the size of the space that counts most; it's what you do with it that really matters! When you look at a small space, close your eyes and then open them again. Ask yourself, "Where is the dead space?" Has every inch of space been used, including areas over doors and around windows? Put up shelves and labeled baskets (which keep the stacks and supplies out of sight) or put up cabinets with semi-clear, semi-frosted doors (which keep supplies in sight so you use them but not so visible that clutter is obvious). Vertical storage means wall shelving or cupboards or over-the-window shelving. Move things around. Put the knickknacks higher up and the tools closer to you. Take down a picture from the wall if it means you can add a cupboard with twelve more linear feet of shelving. If you have children underfoot while you scrapbook, adopt a technique that architects have used for centuries—get a drafting table and work standing up! This keeps the stuff out of reach from most little ones. During this early phase of getting organized, refrain from buying any supplies you will not use within two months! Let the stores dust and keep your paper until you need it. In the meantime, get out the tape measure and note the size of your actual floor and wall space. Then jot down things like how many linear feet of idea magazines and books you own or how big the paper cutter and the Xyron™ really are. Knowing the physical size of your tools and supplies will help you make informed storage purchases.

SOLUTIONS FOR SMALL WORKSPACES

Use these helpful hints to maximize useable space in smaller areas:

- Measure all available floor and wall space, as well as current furnishings. Create a floor plan (see pages 29-31) to help you visualize how furniture and shelving might fit together in a new configuration.

- Base the arrangement of furnishings on the sequential order in which you scrapbook to ensure that what you need most is within easy reach.

- Go vertical with shelving.

- Look for "recovered space" like that under the bed or in closets (see pages 14-15). Store magazines in a window seat or bench shelving.

- Surround windows with shelving and use the window ledge for storage.

- Make decor pull double duty as storage. Measure your supplies so you know what will fit where. Like an artist on a small canvas, make every decorative stroke count!

- Use your corners. Most rooms have four of them. Use triangular storage units to make the most of your corners.

- Use color. Light colors make rooms look larger and dark colors make them look cozier and smaller (see page 20-21).

- Buy only what you need.

- Purge and let go—often! Clean out drawers, files and closets as often as possible. Keep only the best; let go of the rest.

Rule one in small spaces is to go vertical, as Shawna Rendon (Memory Makers Magazine's Idea Editor) has done in her workspace using modular, compartmentalized shelving that extends almost to the ceiling.

To gain a few needed inches of floor space, Jodi Amidei (Craft Editor for Memory Makers Books) cleverly removed her closet doors to accommodate the rolling carts that now fit comfortably in the closet.

Recovering Space From Other Places

Don't forget those under-used rooms or storage areas! Make every inch of your home count so that you have room for your hobby. Shuffling out-of-season items to under-used spaces may free up part of a room elsewhere in the house. Even freeing up a few square feet of space in an unused area of the attic could mean that you now have room to store clutter that had been filling the spare bedroom. Keep an eye out for extra space in every room. Space under stairways can be organized to fit rolling short stack bookcases or shelving. Attics and garages or outbuildings can often be revamped and cleared to make more storage spaces. Some attics and garages have even proven to be airy scrapbooking nooks themselves. Landings, bay window seats, and even large closets can be transformed into places for a scrapbook desk! New closets can be carved out of existing walls with a little elbow grease and carpentry skills. Glean space between existing shelves; excess room between shelves wastes space and decreases the shelves' storage capacity. Rolling under-bed boxes can store multitudes of supplies. Putting the bed up on bedrisers will also give you additional room under the bed. Folding tables can fit behind a headboard or under the bed. Hang pocketed bags behind doors for small tools and punches. No room in the room? Cleaning out a walk-in closet could grant just the space needed for a small desk and a few plastic drawer carts. Look around with a discerning eye. There is space to be had!

Cathy Calvetti's (Eagle River, Wisconsin) scrapbook workspace was formerly an attic in her 1930s saltbox-style home. The sloped ceiling is the perfect height for storing bookcases and shelving beneath it.

When Diane Eppestein (St. Louis, Missouri) and her husband converted a bedroom into a home office, she "staked claim" on the closet for her scrapbook workspace. The closet itself is 90" wide and 24" deep, but the door opening is just 47" wide, leaving about 20" on each side of the bi-fold doors that can be difficult to access. A clever recovery solution for those extra 20" was narrow shelving to store photos, negatives, slides and seldom-used tools. To accommodate the narrow doorway, a drafting table on wheels can be rolled out when access to the shelving is needed. A magnetic board on the back wall holds tools in magnetic baskets as well as photos and pages. Convertible hanging file folders adorn the doors for easy paper access. Diane relies on an Ott-Lite for quality lighting in her small, recovered workspace.

Gabrielle Mader (Whittier, California) recovered two-thirds of the garage from her husband's workspace to call her own. Her husband built her scrapbook workspace from scraps, with all of the comforts of home. The room includes heating and air conditioning, an inlaid light box, a TV, a stereo and a refrigerator. Corkboard surrounds the room where her young daughters often join her to scrapbook. The garage-turned-scrapbook-workspace overlooks the backyard, where Gabrielle can keep an eye on her girls when they're outdoors. Her husband's finishing touch is the under-counter fishing pole "rod" that holds spools of ribbon for scrapbooking and gift wrapping.

Shared or Common Spaces

When your workspace is in the dining room, bedroom, family room or hallway closet, you need to get creative. Think invisible! Invisible means hiding things in baskets, under ottomans, and behind curtains in this shared or public space. Hide what you can from sight for a crisp clean decor. Drawer unit carts and file cabinets that roll away into closets or under desks when not in use are a good bet. Make sure the casters are large and can handle a lot of weight; paper, idea books, punches and rubber stamps are heavy. Armoires are also a popular choice for hiding supplies away from sight. Make empty containers do double duty. Box collections, tins, hat boxes, baskets, jars and linen chests can all be put to work. Storage containers can look like ordinary home decor but *you* will know the truth. Get twice the functionality out of furnishings you already own. A dining table can be your desk. A window seat can be your cozy seating if you add a collapsible card table when needed. Half-empty entertainment centers can store baskets of supplies.

Shared spaces often mean someone will be keeping you company while you work. Keep her comfort in mind. If she likes to scrapbook, make sure there is table space for her and a comfortable extra chair. Keeping a snack or two on hand is nice as long as things don't get messy. A favorite toy and nice floor mat might be a nice addition if your scrapbooking buddy is a child. Scrapbooking harmony in shared spaces might be easier than you think!

SAFETY CONSIDERATIONS

Keep safety considerations in mind when moving your scrapbook supplies into a shared space. Keep potentially harmful items—such as adhesive remover, embossing powders, preservation sprays, stamp cleaners, glitter and sharp tools—out of reach of small children. Secure wire racks and bookcases to the walls. Use ventilation when working with heat embossing and sprays. Heat guns and corded tools should be unplugged and put away on upper shelving after each use. Heavy tools like paper trimmers and die-cut machines need to be away from countertop edges so they don't get pulled down by accident. Look at your space and tools just as you would a garage, workshop or kitchen. Keep it safe, particularly where children are concerned.

DISGUISING YOUR SCRAPBOOK WORKSPACE

Do you want to disguise your scrapbooking space? Curtained shelving and roll-top units disguise the mess for you. They also keep busy little hands off your work between sessions. Floor screens or wall dividers can help set room boundaries and hide clutter at the same time. Try to get file cabinets and shelving in the same wood tones as other furnishings in the room. For example, if you scrap in your dining room, and your dining table is cherry, go for a cherry finish on the paper or tool drawer units. Maintaining the same tones in wood finish lessens the visual impact of your "work" furniture in a "non-work" room.

Tracy Wynn's (Truro, Nova Scotia, Canada) closet scrapbook workspace shares common ground with her home's spare bedroom/computer office— a fairly common scenario. To conceal her workspace from the rest of the multi-function room, Tracy simply draws the curtains closed.

Christy Baker's (Pleasant Hill, Missouri) multipurpose basement playroom/scrapbook workspace live together harmoniously thanks to Christy's great organizational skills for both her "toys" as well as her children's. Christy didn't have to spend a lot to get organized; much of her furniture and shelving was either salvaged from trash, recycled from other areas of the house or handmade by her husband. And with such a colorful and well-stocked play area, the kids have no need to get into Christy's scrapbook supplies!

Jenna Beegle's (Woodstock, Georgia) kitchen scrapbook nook sits at one end of the busiest room in the home. The kitchen's dining area was converted to functional workspace with kitchen cabinets and countertop to match her existing fixtures. Jenna's chair is on the other side of the countertop. Shelving was built into the window seat to increase storage space.

Three storage products that work great in shared spaces are Lifetime's® Personal Table that folds, Charming Ideas' clip-on Table-Pal™ that rolls up and Jokari's 24-pocket Scrap'N Stor™ over-the-door system.

Office-type hutches that close after you're done scrapbooking are a fine solution for scrapbooking in shared spaces. Simply open the doors, pull up a chair and you're ready to scrapbook. Shown are For Keeps Sake's Creation Station and two rolling companion KeepsSake Carts. Collectors Cabinets also produces a line of pine and oak cabinetry that blends well with other furniture in shared spaces.

Creating a Plan of Action • 17

Workspace Essentials

Scrapbookers vary in what they feel are the absolute essentials for an effective workspace. However, some basics seem to be universal. You can adapt this list as you see fit. Make sure your work area has what you need on hand, in good supply and that supplies and tools are within arm's reach if possible.

Once you know what the basic workspace essentials are, evaluate the furnishings that you own. Will they provide you with the space you need to work? Is there room for growth? Will you be comfortable sitting for long periods of time? Is the lighting adequate? Will you have enough shelving? Answering these and other questions will help you make wise decisions when determining if you need to purchase additional furnishings to make the space work for you. Use the ideas that follow as a starting point for creating a comfortable workspace with room for growth.

A productive scrapbook workspace features essential basics like those shown here: Sturdi-Craft modular cabinets, drawer units, pegboard and ample work surface and shelving; Daylight's Scrapbook Lamp™; The Board Dudes' combination cork/magnetic bulletin board; Ergonomic Services' ergonomically correct chair and Rubbermaid's trash can.

DESKTOP

Tabletop or desk workspace surface should measure at least three square feet but the bigger the better. Keep in mind that you can store seldom-used tools such as large paper trimmers, adhesive application machines and die-cut machines on separate countertops or sturdy tables elsewhere. Get in the mindset that your desk should stay clear except for the page you are currently working on. The surface should be smooth and easy to wipe clean. If possible, leave room for a friend to work beside or across from you. Sometimes it is nice to crop with a buddy.

FILING

You will need some sort of filing system. A file cabinet, a desk drawer, or a portable accordion file or rolling cart will all store idea sheets, poems and quotes, receipts, sticker sheets, page additions and other 8½ x 11" paperwork in file folders.

LIGHT

Let there be light, and plenty of it! Good lighting can increase your productivity from 10 to 40 percent and can decrease neck strain, mistakes and headaches. Good lighting allows you to accurately see photo colors and select papers and page accents that will coordinate beautifully. Light also affects your mood. You will need good light not only in the daytime but at night, too. Make sure the lighting you have is clear, natural light. Several light manufacturers make this kind of bulb, which is readily available at hobby and discount stores. Good light is especially important in northern climates, in the evening hours or if you have seasonal affective disorder. Everyday lamps and fixtures are fine—just make sure they have the right kind of bulbs in them. Ideally, your work light should come from above your shoulders or from the side onto your work surface. Avoid glare by changing the angle of the light or decreasing the wattage of the bulb. Counteract direct sunlight that causes glare with sheer curtains or semi-sheer blinds.

POWER

Where are the power outlets? Where is the phone? Orient your workspace around some of these important elements. Cords should not run across walking paths. Generally, it is good to have at least one outlet within five feet of your space. Electricity should be accessible for both accent room lighting and your tools. Easy access to other electronics, such as a computer or radio, are also important considerations.

SEATING

Most scrapbookers sit while they work. Get a good chair that is right for you. An adjustable chair is best so that you can change it to suit your height. This will help you avoid neck strain and backache. Cushions are nice; swivels are optional. If your room is carpeted and you want to use a rolling chair, consider getting a plastic office floor mat like those used in office settings. Test drive a chair in the store before you buy it. Make yours as comfortable as possible.

SHELVING

Give every tool its own place. Use shelving or space for paper, books, tools, and other supplies. Shelving comes in all shapes and sizes, from wood bookcases to wire cubes. Make sure you have the size and space you need and that the shelves will bear the weight and suit the dimensions of your intended stock items. Measure first, buy or build second.

TRASH CAN

Not only does scrapbooking come with a lot of tools and supplies, it tends to create a lot of refuse. Keep your work area clean by having a trash can or trash bags handy.

VENTILATION

Safety is of primary importance. Ventilation and heat are also important aspects to consider. Fumes and excessive heat are not good for you or your photos and paper.

WALL SPACE

Posting notes, ideas, and small supplies up on a bulletin board or pegboard in front of you will save table space and keep clutter off the work surface. Invest in a bulletin board or pegboard if you have space for it.

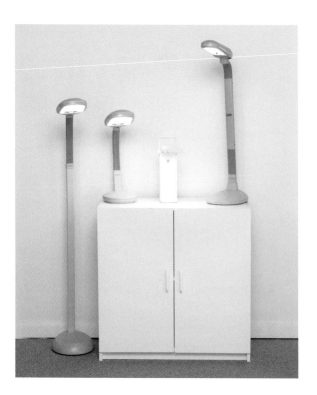

Quality, natural lighting provides true color rendition when matching photo colors to those in paper, pre-made page accents, embellishments and colorants. It's also easier on the eyes when scrapbooking for an extended period of time. Some favored scrapbook lamps include (left to right): Verilux's HappyEyes™ Floor and Desk Lamps, Daylight's Compact Lamp and Ott-Lite® Technology's TrueColor™ FlexArm Plus Lamp. Be sure to check out these manufacturer Web sites as models and styles differ widely to suit your personal workspace needs.

Room Colors for Enhanced Creativity

If you are fortunate enough to have an entire room dedicated to scrapbooking, one of the most fun aspects of getting organized can be selecting the color for your walls. Two key points to consider when deciding the color of your workspace are your personality and the work that you'll be doing in the room.

Choosing a color sounds simple enough, but many people don't realize the impact the color of a room can have on the work that's done there. So when poring over the endless palette of paint chips and color swatches at your local paint store, keep in mind that the primary color you select could possibly act as a "creative enhancer" for your workspace. Whichever colors you choose to personalize your workspace, remember that it's your space and should reflect your personality while inspiring you to be creative.

WHITE

White lends itself to, and blends with, the countless moods and colors used in scrapbooking. Don't fret about white being dull or lifeless. Rather, it can be fresh and crisp one moment and pure and soft the next. White represents freshness and a clean slate. A white background offers no distractions to the project at hand. This "non-color" makes walls appear to recede, giving the illusion of a larger room. With white as a base color, you'll be able to change accent colors as often as you like.

COLOR INSPIRATION

Walk through your home, spending some time in each room—particularly in your favorite places. Observe your feelings, then notice the colors around you. You'll find that certain colors inspire specific emotions. Check out some books on using color in the home to better understand the energy created by different colors. With these insights you're ready to choose the colors to accent your workspace while staying true to your personality. Here's more color for thought:

The white walls of Kimberly Ling's (Fresno, California) scrapbook room make her tools, supplies, mementos and trinkets "pop" from their perches on the walls for quick visibility and access. Note Kimberly's interesting use of her desk's keyboard tray; she uses it to store punches!

COOL COLORS

A splash of blue soothes and relaxes with its optimism. Pale and dusty blues appear delicate, while cobalt, turquoise and aquamarine can bring a room electric vitality. Some blues, however, can give a room a chilly effect. Green, nature's neutral, forms a refreshing, almost spiritual backdrop for a scrapbook workspace. Easy-going green provides a quick pick-me-up in many of its countless shades. Purple infuses sporty playfulness in its various shades and hues.

Katie Schwetz's (St. Louis, Missouri) cool (in many ways!) blue and green scrapbook workspace sings with invigorating expectancy. Even the painted pegboard seems alive and ready to help!

WARM COLORS

Flashy and dramatic red lends passion, energy and vitality to a workspace. Darker reds emit timeless elegance, while pale pinks add a touch of gentle femininity. Bright reds and hot pinks can be overpowering; use in small doses. Shades of orange can bring a warm robustness and excitement to the workspace, while peach provides a sense of peacefulness. The optimistic attitude of yellow raises the spirits and brings a sense of warmth and joy to help you stay focused.

Debby Schuh's (Williamsville, New York) bright, rose-red walls give her workspace spirit and spunk while Gina Will's (Arlington Heights, Illinois) yellow workspace glows with cozy, welcoming ambiance.

The Ergonomic Workspace

We've all heard of tennis elbow, but what about cropper's elbow? Or cropper's neck, back, hands and eyes, for that matter. If you spend even a few hours at a time cropping, you've no doubt endured crop-related pain. That pain can slow you down, or worse, develop into a chronic injury.

Croppers are susceptible to several injuries that can affect the hands, wrists and back. Incorrect posture and repetitive and forceful tasks cause tendons, muscles and nerve tissue excessive wear and tear.

Croppers typically practice risky postures while crafting: hunched shoulders; bent/flexed wrists; repetitive hand, arm and shoulder motions; long reaches for materials; long periods of sitting and on nonadjustable chairs; working with the neck bent and using pinched grips on pens, pencils and cutting tools.

The good news is that simple changes in your posture and workspace or workstation setup will make noticeable differences, says Brian Foxhoven, certified ergonomic evaluator and owner of Ergonomic Services, Inc.

When Foxhoven evaluates a workstation, he identifies factors that put people at risk of injury and then recommends the proper adjustments. He pointed out the following factors and suggested changes after observing and evaluating scrapbookers at work.

This is an ergonomically correct cropper. Take note of the following:
1. *The lumbar area, or lower back, is supported, and the cropper exhibits neutral back, shoulder and neck posture.*
2. *The crop station is at forearm level to keep wrists straight and neutral.*
3. *The hips are slightly higher than the knees.*
4. *The knees are bent at a 90-degree angle.*
5. *Feet are flat and a footrest is utilized to compensate for short stature.*
6. *Task lighting exists to reduce eyestrain.*

POSTURE

Posture-related changes will almost instantly make your body feel better, Foxhoven says. "Ergonomics is fitting the workstation to the body, so evaluating posture is key," he says. "The workstation or workspace setup will be different for everyone."

Height and weight determine the correct workstation setup. Guidelines for correct crop-station posture are as follows: The back should be straight with a slight, supported curve in the lumbar, or lower back, region. The neck and wrists are straight. Shoulders are relaxed. Hips are parallel to the floor, and knees are bent at a 90-degree angle. Feet rest flat. The work surface sits more or less at forearm height. All furniture is big or small enough to suit the individual's stature.

REPETITION

Repetition is the hardest risk factor to control when constant cutting, craft-knife work and trimming need to be done. It can increase strain and pressure on the joints, tendons, blood vessels and nerves. Repetitive movements can lead to injuries like Carpal Tunnel Syndrome, which causes tingling, numbness and weakness in the wrists. The most effective way to reduce repetition is to vary your tasks and to take breaks, Foxhoven says. Set an egg timer to remind yourself to switch jobs, or better yet, take frequent breaks—10 minutes each hour.

Breaks also increase productivity. Use precut products, die-cut titles or torn-paper accents to reduce the amount of cutting and trimming.

FORCE

Narrow tools, like a craft knife, and slick work surfaces cause one to naturally increase force. Force tightens muscles that then decrease the blood flow to tissue, causing lactic acid buildup.

If your knuckles turn white when you cut with your craft knife, something needs to change. Alter your grip or try using rubber grips on your knives, pens and pencils to reduce finger force. The Pencil Grip's grips (shown below) increase a narrow tool's surface area, making it easier to hold.

Several companies create products with an ergonomic edge to help reduce force (see below). The McGill Strongarm is a press that reduces the amount of force necessary to activate a punch, thereby enabling children and arthritics to punch easier.

The Quickutz Personal Die-Cutting System acts like a desk press. By resting the hand tool in a cradle, scrapbookers use their weight to precision-cut letters and shapes.

You can also reduce force by performing tasks such as punching and stamping while standing to use stronger muscle groups.

Ergonomic scrapbooking products

1. Tutto Bag Tylenol and the Arthritis Foundation bestowed a design award on this bag for being back-friendly. It's easy to pull and maneuver, and it's versatile and durable.

2. Footrest Shorter croppers can keep their feet flat with a footrest, like this one from McGill, Inc.

3. Pencil/knife grips Grips increase the contact area on narrow tools, like pens and craft knives. These are from The Pencil Grip.

4. Lumbar pillow Strap this lumbar pillow to a chair to support the lower back. Check back stores and the Internet for one that suits you.

5. Daylight Task Light Proper light reduces eyestrain and promotes good posture. It also eliminates glare and shadows.

6. Strongarm Punch The Strongarm from McGill reduces the amount of force needed to punch.

7. Fiskars scissors Soft Touch scissors are spring-loaded to ease the force used for repetitive cutting action.

8. QuicKutz To operate this personal die-cutting system, place the tool into the desk cradle and use body weight to precision-cut letters and shapes.

DESIGNING THE ERGONOMIC WORKSPACE

Your scrapbook workspace should be designed to fit your body in its most neutral position. A neutral position exists at the halfway point in a joint's range of motion. Use the following tips to adjust your workstation to fit you.

The chair is the best tool for addressing posture, so it's worth it to invest in a quality chair. Look for a chair with adjustable height (a pneumatic lift) and adjustable back tilt. A few dollars today translates into pennies for a lifetime of proper sitting.

The chair's seat pan should be shallow or deep enough to fit your body. When sitting back, two or three fingers should fit between the back of the knee and the edge of the seat. Also, get a chair without arm rests. Arm rests hinder cropping and promote unnatural arm posture, causing stress on the shoulders.

When seated at the workstation, pull the chair as close to the table as possible to keep the lumbar region supported. If you are going to a crop and cannot bring your chair, try a lumbar-support pillow that straps onto the back of the chair, or a rolled-up towel.

While maintaining the natural curve of the spine, sit at a slight forward angle, Foxhoven advises. You can sit on a pillow to increase chair height or use a seat wedge pillow that also promotes the slightly forward posture recommended for scrapbooking.

A secondary risk factor related to posture is contact stress. Contact stress occurs when an object presses into the body, cutting off circulation and causing discomfort. Shorter legs may go numb because the seat edge inflicts contact stress on dangling legs. A footrest will keep feet flat. McGill makes a heated footrest. Telephone books can also serve the same purpose.

Using a task light instead of overhead light also promotes good posture by reducing eyestrain. Overhead light, or indirect light, either hits the back of the head and casts shadows over your work or bounces off the work surface and causes a glare. A task light provides direct light over your work, reducing eyestrain and the need to hunch over in order to see your work. Beware of bright, natural light from windows. This also causes glare.

If possible, work on an angle to reduce glare. Portable, angled desk easels that rest on top of your crop table raise work a few inches, making it easier to keep your neck and shoulders straight. You can set the desk easel aside if a certain task requires a horizontal surface.

Redesign tasks to suit your neutral posture. For example, if trimming with a craft knife, position the paper so you are cutting toward your body with your wrist straight, instead of cutting in the direction across your body with a bent wrist. The same can apply when using a paper trimmer.

Use these practical solutions to improve your posture and to cut back on repetitive movements and the use of force. By reducing the risk factors, you increase your productivity, which leads to another solution: More pages in less time!

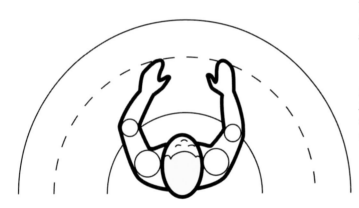

Keep supplies around you in a semicircle—within the Easy Reach Zone. Supplies used most frequently should be the closest to you; supplies seldom used should be farthest. Organize tools and supplies from left to right, or right to left, in the order in which you use them.

Top ten tips for healthier scrapbooking

1. Vary tasks and take breaks to increase productivity. Set a timer to remind you to take short breaks.

2. Incorporate stretches and exercises into your crops. Visit ctdnews.com/suffer/CTDprevent.html for a list of easy and effective exercises. Build up muscle groups that feel the effects of scrapbooking, like the shoulders and hands.

3. Use tools that decrease force whenever possible.

4. Support the lower back with a lumbar pillow or rolled-up towel.

5. Use a footrest or phone book to help keep feet flat.

6. Increase task lighting to alleviate eyestrain.

7. Use different workstations for different tasks. Use sitting stations for precise work, like beading, and standing stations for force-intensive work, like punching or stamping, to permit more efficient use of the upper body.

8. Keep often-used tools and supplies within the "swing space," or within the Easy Reach Zone (see above illustration).

9. Orient your work to suit you whenever possible. Redesign the task to keep your body in a neutral position.

10. Work at forearm level to keep arms, neck and shoulders relaxed and wrists straight and neutral.

Budget Considerations

Even if you're on a tight budget, you already have four assets to help you acquire the space you need and the storage solutions you crave. Don't underestimate the following resources.

ATTITUDE

If you're willing to change, you must be willing to work. The first resource you need is attitude, which will drive how successful your organizational efforts turn out to be. Don't delay! Make time for this project and get started. Ensure organizational success with these tips:

• Get ready to change what is needed—inside and out.

• Make a plan. This book will give you the tools you need to complete the task and do it right. Purchase items you need so your budget doesn't take a big hit all at once.

• Be realistic. Perfection is not the goal. Gaining an efficient workspace and a method of organization that works for you is the goal. Just because you can't afford $3,000 built-in shelves doesn't mean you can't start getting organized. Begin with small things and persevere. Bit by bit it will all get done.

• Do your homework. Assess your budget. What funds, if any, are available for this project? Use the convenient products and ideas featured in this book as a starting point and check on their prices. You'll find the companies that manufacture these products listed in the Source Guide at the back of this book.

• Keep your system going. For most, this means simply putting things back in their places. Doing a little every day goes a long way to feeling organized. Maintaining the system you set up is more important than unlimited budgets or highly specialized containers.

BUDGET

Is the sky the limit? Probably not. But do take stock of your organization project budget and the monetary resources available. What changes can you truly afford to make? What solutions can be saved for someday in the future? Can you use a secondhand desk until the next pay raise? Will a set of bookcases from the basement do in the short term? Make a list of what work items you truly need right now and what can wait (see page 28). Consider nice-looking modular furniture or shelving to which you can add units over time. Search out easy-to-construct shelving plans online or in simple woodworking books. A little elbow grease goes a long way toward creating a space you will use and love.

Truly assess your budget and the monetary resources you might have as well as determine what furniture and storage containers you have and those you need for a logical approach to getting organized without "losing your shirt."

If you are on a budget, plan your expenditures. Create a budget work sheet or use the one on the following page, then do your homework and save. A few dollars set aside a week will soon add up to buy your larger items. There are still plenty of ways to organize your space using what you have on hand. Do-it-yourself options abound for workspaces. Don't be put off by the high cost of special furnishings or organizational solutions. Simply ask yourself whether you have a container that will fit certain supplies. If the answer is yes, go get it and start using it now. You can always make a list of items you want to buy later on. Don't let tight finances stop you from finding solutions—even if they are short-term solutions.

UNDERUTILIZED FURNISHINGS

You may already own home furnishings that will work in your new space. Most families have an extra dresser, table and chair in storage somewhere just waiting to be called into use again. Check attics, garages, basements and each room in the home for little-used items that can be used in your scrapbook workspace. Ask friends and family to see if they have something useful. A few common furnishings "found" around the house might include bookcases, bulletin boards, chairs, desks, file cabinets, lamps, shelving and tables. See pages 88-89 for "found" storage containers.

PEOPLE

Take stock of the human resources around you. Can you put these resources to work for you? Do you have time to do the organization yourself or would you gladly pay someone to plan and organize your space? Does your dad work in a cabinet shop? Is your cousin a closet organizer? Is your spouse a great woodworker? Maybe your mom is available to baby-sit weekly, freeing you up to tackle organizational chores. Ask them to help you or trade their expertise for some of your own. Perhaps someone you know would gladly make you a shelf unit in exchange for getting his or her photos organized chronologically. It doesn't hurt to ask!

Scrapbook Workspace Budget Considerations

This work sheet can help you create and track a workspace-improvement budget. Fill in the blanks as you do your planning and research. If estimated costs are higher than actual costs on certain items, consider saving these purchases for a later date as more funds become available.

BEGINNING DATE		
ENDING DATE		
PERSONAL BUDGET		
WORKSPACE NEEDS	**ESTIMATED COST**	**ACTUAL COST**
DESK		
CHAIR		
LIGHT		
BOOKCASE		
SHELVING		
TOTALS		

Paring Down

By now, you have analyzed your workspace options. You have a good idea of what workspace essentials involve: a large work surface, quality lighting, a comfortable chair, wall and shelf space, and filing space. You've examined potential room colors for enhanced creativity and understand what constitutes an "ergonomically safe" workspace. You have even worked out any budget considerations. With all of this "homework" completed, now is the time to pare down any plans that may prove too costly including new furniture and large-item storage container purchases. Determine the first changes you will make to your physical workspace. The work sheet on the following page will help you with this phase of getting organized.

Begin by reviewing your Budget Consideration work sheet. Use a critical decision-making process before acquiring any new furnishings. Collect magazine and Internet photos of furniture or storage items that you like and note their precise dimensions. The worst thing you can do is to buy something that will not fit your budget, your workspace or your belongings.

Decide what additional pieces and changes you need to make in order to function better in your scrapbook workspace. The general storage rule of thumb is that you usually need at least twice as much storage space as you believe.

There are a number of things you can do to pare down your workspace plans if they seem too far-fetched. Empty and clean newly acquired used furniture, shelving and file cabinets. Even if you don't like the look of these items, they can serve their purpose in the interim. Put off building those cabinets for now and give yourself time to save money for them. Consider purchasing modular furniture and storage units that you can add to over the course of time.

Remember to keep your focus on organization, not acquisition. Make only those necessary furnishings purchases that will help you achieve your goal. All in good time, your dream space will emerge.

ScrapNCube's flexible furniture, including its line of Cubit! modular units, can be configured in a myriad of ways. The units can be purchased all at once or a little at a time as your budget allows and your supplies grow.

Display Dynamic's modular furniture components can also be combined in various configurations as budgets allow. Shown are the company's Scrapbook Station (above) and Mobile File with Slide-Out Tray (right).

Developing a Step-by-Step Plan of Action

Based on what you have learned in the previous pages, analyze and evaluate your existing workspace situation and belongings to discover what you need in order to make immediate progress in getting organized. These questions will help you strategize and create a specific plan of action.

1. Do you like the furniture you have and why?	7. What kind of furniture would you like to add?
2. What kind of space do you have to work with?	8. What changes would you like to make?
3. What does your furniture contribute to the way you scrapbook?	9. Do you want to have your computer right on your scrapbook workspace?
4. Do you have adequate shelving or room to add shelving?	10. If there's not enough room, where else might you put the computer so it's still handy?
5. What furniture do you want to keep?	11. What changes can you afford to make?
6. How would you describe the quality of your workspace lighting?	12. What changes do you plan for the future?

How to Create a Floor Plan

Whether you have a shared space or an entire room devoted to scrapbooking, it can be beneficial to create a floor plan (or drawing) early in your organizational project. A floor plan helps you visualize a room before you start moving furniture around. Desks and cabinets can be heavy, so before you lift and move them, it's nice to know ahead of time their best placement.

A floor plan also contains essential facts that will prove useful on shopping trips to scrapbook, craft and furniture stores. With a floor plan and a tape measure, you will be able to measure and select new furnishings and storage vessels to ensure they will fit into your workspace scheme.

Floor plans are so useful that learning how to draw them is among the first things taught in many interior design classes. Drawings of your scrapbook workspace needn't be beautiful and artistic renderings; simple sketches—drawn to scale—will do fine. Move paper cutouts that represent your furnishings around on a scaled drawing of your workspace. It's fun, easy and quite informative!

SKETCH

Begin by sketching a rough drawing of your scrapbook workspace's floor or wall dimensions. You needn't worry about scale yet; simply draw a representation and rough sketch of the room. Show the approximate shape and size of the space, together with any connecting doors, closets, hallways, or permanent fixtures, such as built-in bookcases or shelving.

MEASURE

Using a steel tape measure, begin at one corner of the room or space and measure the distance to the opposite corner. Record that measurement on your rough sketch. Continue measuring each wall of the workspace and recording measurements. Measure twice and record once for accuracy. If your tape measure slips or moves, ask a spouse, child or friend to help, or use masking tape to hold the tape measure securely in place.

Next, measure any connecting doors, hallways, or permanent fixtures, such as built-in bookcases or shelving, as well as the height beneath windows if these spaces will be used for storage or furniture. Measure closet dimensions if you plan on outfitting a closet for storage.

SCALE

Now transfer your workspace or room to ½" scale using quad-ruled (4 squares equal one-half inch, which equals one foot of actual space) graph paper, a pencil or pen and a clear plastic graphing ruler. Some interior designers draw floor plans in ¼" scale (¼" on paper equals one foot of actual space) and there are office and home furnishings templates available in ¼" scale if you prefer working in this smaller size. At ½" scale size, you can fit most rooms on a single sheet of graph paper with enough room in the margins to make notations. This latter scale size is easier to work with if you've never created floor plan because the drawings are larger.

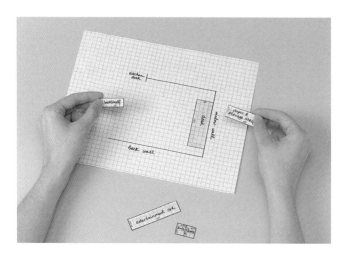

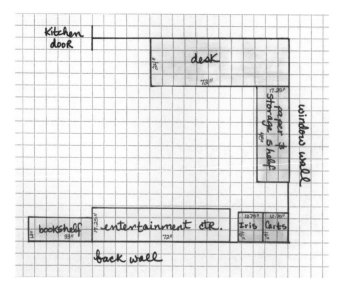

By moving representational paper cutouts of furniture around on a scaled-down drawing of your scrapbook workspace, you will get a good visual idea of which arrangements are worth trying (top). When you shuffle the paper patterns around until you feel comfortable with the organization of the furnishings, a working blueprint develops for the workspace (center). The blueprint plan then springs to life as you arrange your furniture and shelving according to your floor plan (bottom). Scrapbook workspace photo courtesy of Cori Dahmen (Portland, Oregon).

Use the graphing ruler to create straight lines on the graph paper, to help maintain 90-degree angle corners and to draw accurate line length. Keep in mind that two grid boxes on the quad-ruled graph paper represent one foot of actual space.

It can be difficult to mark inches or anything less than one foot on your scale drawing. For these, you will have to mark portions of grid boxes on the graphing paper, perhaps even "eye-balling" it before marking. For example, at ½" scale, two inches would be one-third of a grid box. Strive for accuracy whenever possible to ensure that the furnishings you have and those you intend to purchase will actually fit in your workspace.

Record any connecting doors, hallways, or permanent fixtures, such as built-in bookcases or shelving, as well as the height beneath windows if you plan to use the space for storage or furniture. Transfer closet dimensions if you plan on outfitting a closet for storage as well.

FURNISHINGS

Use a tape measure to measure the width of any furniture or storage units that will go along the walls of your workspace. In your measurements, allow for room between units or for walkways if needed. In addition, measure the height of any furniture or storage units that will go beneath windows and the depth of any storage units that you may be placing in a closet. Before you make any new storage unit purchases, make a trip to the store to get their measurements.

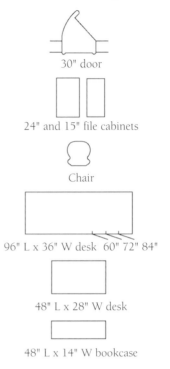

Furniture & floor plan shapes

30" door

24" and 15" file cabinets

Chair

96" L x 36" W desk   60" 72" 84"

48" L x 28" W desk

48" L x 14" W bookcase

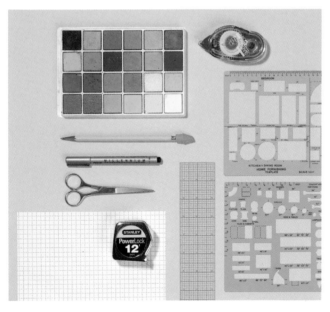

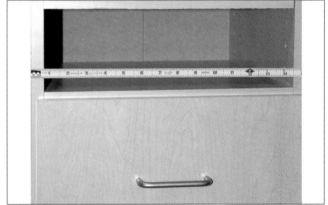

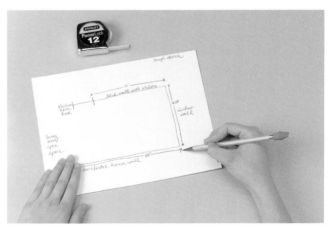

To create a floor plan, you'll need the following tools (above): quad-ruled (4 squares = 1") graph paper, a pencil, an eraser, a clear graphing ruler and a tape measure. Use the key above to freehand draw furniture and room shapes or use office and home furnishings templates (C-Thru Ruler Company) to create shapes for placement on your floor plan. Use a tape measure to measure the width and depth of furniture (above right) as well as the physical floor space of your area. Use the scale of ½" equals 1' of actual size to create the floor plan. Before making a scaled-down floor plan, sketch a rough drawing (right) of the room's shape, jotting down the measurements of any walls, windows and doors that will be part of your workspace.

Use additional graph paper to create the paper cutouts representative of the furniture and storage containers you intend to keep in your scrapbook workspace, transferring your measurements as accurately as possible to the grids on the graph paper. Trace around the shapes in black pen and color with chalk if desired. Use scissors to cut out the paper shapes of your mock furniture.

CREATE THE FLOOR PLAN

Now for the fun part! Move the paper cutouts around against the walls of your paper floor plan. Think about how you scrapbook as it applies to the intended use of the furniture and storage units, and arrange the items accordingly. Leave plenty of room for pathways, moving your chair side to side or forward and back, opening file drawers and closet doors, etc.

Take your time. And don't be discouraged if you don't get it "just right" on the first attempt. When you discover the perfect arrangement, you'll know it.

When you're happy with a final arrangement, use a removable adhesive to glue the paper cutouts in place on the floor plan. That way, if you discover some inaccurate measuring or something just doesn't fit like you had hoped, you can move the shapes around on the floor plan again.

Put your plan into action by physically moving the furniture and storage units you have on hand into the places noted on the floor plan. Then take your floor plan and a tape measure shopping with you to buy new furniture or storage units.

With a plan like this, you're sure to create a functional and effective workspace with minimal backache and budget pain!

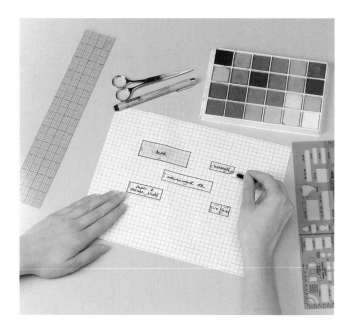

Again, using the scale of ½" to equal 1' of actual size, use a pen and graphing ruler to freehand draw (or use the furnishings templates to trace at ¼" scale) the paper pattern cutouts to represent your furnishings. These paper patterns don't have to be precise, but getting them as close to accurate as possible will ensure that your furnishings actually fit into your workspace in the way that you envision them. Taking accurate measurements will help achieve this goal.

Recommended spacing

Use the following spacing guidelines to help you create a functional floor plan that maximizes your space yet still gives you room to move about as freely as possible:

Foot-traffic walkways

36" in busy, shared spaces; 24" to 30" in private or seldom-used spaces

Chair pull-back and side-to-side space

About 36" to 40"; 42" if the space is also a foot-traffic walkway

In front of desks

36" for standing room while opening drawers; 42" to 60" for pulling back chair

Between desk, cabinets, bookshelves

These items can butt up against each other or you can leave room to squeeze bins, racks or drawer units between them

In front of filing cabinets

Allow enough room for drawers to extend fully

In front of closets and bookshelves

36" to view contents if doors slide or fold open; width of closet doors if they swing open

Between wall shelves

Height between shelves should accommodate the tallest items you will store on the shelves; allow head space so you don't bump your head when standing

TAKING STOCK I: NON-CONSUMABLE TOOLS & SUPPLIES

Getting organized may seem like a less daunting task now that the workspace itself is more in order and ready to receive your tools and supplies. You may be surrounded now by messy piles of photos, memorabilia and scrapbooking tools. Perhaps your digital files are out of control as well, making it time-consuming to search for the fonts and images when you need them. Take heart, step back for a minute and breathe.

In this chapter, you will be gathering, sorting, cleaning, repairing and labeling your non-consumable items. Perhaps you'll even decide to purge, donate or sell items you no longer use. You will learn how to master the "divide & conquer, clean & label" theory. It is a process that you will repeat over and over again while getting organized, regardless of the type of tool or supply you are getting under control.

The time you spend now will ensure that these items serve you for a long, long time. Keep what works for you. Do a little at a time. Gradually it won't be such a daunting task to look at that photo stack or that tool bin. You will know exactly where every item is when you need it. Each step along the way will bring focus back to your scrapbooking area and to your goals for the hobby.

The "Divide & Conquer, Clean & Label" Theory

This theory is a simple process that will help you get organized. Use this "plan of attack" regardless of what type of tools or supplies you are organizing. You will first gather all of one type of item together. Then you will divide it into piles for "keeping" and "getting rid of." Next, you will clean and repair the keepers and either donate, sell or regift the unwanted items. Before storing the keepers, be sure to label the items as well as the drawer, box or bin they will be stored in. That way, you will know where they are at a glance and any item that might accompany you to a future crop will be labeled with your name or your initials.

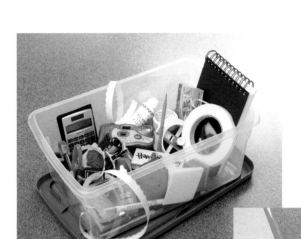

Empty storage areas, bins and drawers of scrapbook supplies and gather in one place. Sort and group like items; determine what to get rid of. Clean and label the keepers so they're ready for use and for cropping on the go.

Keep a good supply of labels, index cards and dividers, binder dividers and sticky notes handy for labeling your "keepers." Dymo's Letra Tag QX50 is a user- and cost-friendly labeling system that can help you create a unified look among your labeled tools and supplies.

Top five ways to rid yourself of unwanted tools & supplies

Donate them

Give your tools and supplies to a charitable organization, such as a school, church group, baby-sitting co-op, the Picture Me Foundation, Girl or Boy Scouts of America, a nursing home or a children's hospital.

Swap them

Set unwanted items aside for a future in-home or Internet swap (see following page).

Sell them

Sell the items at a garage sale or the flea market. List items in a local newspaper ad or sell them on an Internet auction. For a minimal fee, some local scrapbook stores may allow you to display your wares on select days.

Regift them

Give the items to your children to help them foster a love for preserving memories or wrap the items up for a special scrapbooking friend.

Discard them

If the items are simply beyond repair, toss them out for good.

How to host a swap

As you go through the process of dividing, conquering, cleaning and labeling, you'll inevitably run across items perfect for a swap. Swapping one unwanted item for an item you will use can help you recoup some of your original cost. You can also make an outright sale of your item at the swap if you can't find anything to trade for that you will use. Don't bring home any swapped items that you won't use. For a successful swap, try these tips:

In-Home Swaps

- Send out invitations at least 2-3 weeks in advance.
- Create plenty of open space with comfortable seating.
- Provide large tables for displaying supplies. Supply price tags and pens.
- Offer refreshments.
- Provide tally sheets for guests to keep track of trades or purchases.
- Make the atmosphere festive with table decorations and music.

Internet swaps

- Join an online group and be a part of the fun.
- Determine the style of the swap; for example, try a "round robin" swap.
- Select the type of items to be swapped; for example, swap page additions or, perhaps, cutting tools.
- E-mail information regarding your intentions to host a swap to interested parties.
- Provided a complete set of rules to all swappers.
- Remind participants to include correct postage on their swap parcels or shipping boxes.
- E-mail sender a notice of confirmation upon receipt.

- Regularly post the status of the swap on the appropriate Internet bulletin board.
- Be punctual in sending swapped materials to participants.
- Check out these Internet Web sites for more information on swaps: www.scrapbook.com, www.havilandtelco.com, www.ourlittlesiteontheweb.com and www.twopeasinabucket.com.

Swapping one unwanted item for an item you will use can help you recoup some of your original cost. Just don't trade for or bring home any swapped items you won't use or you'll set yourself back in the goal of getting organized.

Taming Our Most Prized Possessions

Scrapbooking involves getting your most prized possessions, such as photos, negatives and memorabilia—even slides, computer files, digital images, audio and visual images and sounds—into safe storage environments so that you can utilize and enjoy them for years to come. While these cherished and irreplaceable possessions are the heart and soul of scrapbooking, they are also the most difficult to get under control because of the sheer volume of these items. Over the years, the "piles" get bigger and bigger. With a good organizational system, even an unruly mountain of memories can be tamed.

Photographs

Negligence harms photos the most. Left in piles and bundles and crammed into drawers, they crumple and get brittle. Unsorted photos get lost. Undocumented photos get thrown away. Each year that photos are left unattended and unsafe, their demise is hastened. With some sound advice, your photos will become easily accessible while stored in the safest of all possible environments.

CARE

To care for your photos, you must recognize—and avoid—the top threats to photo longevity. You can deal with each threat in a positive way. Each photo care challenge has its own solution.

- Humidity can wreak havoc on precious photos. Emulsions shift, mildew grows, photos start to warp, and pages stick together. According to the Library of Congress, humidity is the greatest enemy of photographic materials. The ideal storage humidity is between 20-50 percent humidity. If your rooms exceed this, you can purchase desiccant crystals from major photo suppliers. These crystals will absorb excess humidity from a room.

- Consistent storage temperatures are important. Ideal conditions for photo storage is in the range of 60-75 degrees Fahrenheit. If you have a cool basement that is not humid, this is ideal. Never store photos in an attic. Attics are the worst rooms in the home for temperature fluctuation. Steady temperature is especially important to color photographs because of their chemical compositions. Repeated cold temperatures make photo chemicals less stable. Try not to let your photos freeze. Do not leave them in the car if you live in excessively cold, hot and/or humid climates.

Sooner or later, we all have a stockpile of unorganized photos, negatives and memorabilia just begging for organization and, ultimately, to be put in a scrapbook album so their stories can be told.

- pH levels are also important. In chemical terms, acid also harms photos. A severe base compound would also be harmful. Photos want to be neutral. The safe range for photos is 7.5-8.5 pH level. Use only albums, papers, pens and embellishments that are made from durable and chemically stable materials. Paper should also be acid- and lignin-free. Check with a pH acid testing pen if in doubt about any scrapbooking or storage product.

- Avoid unsafe plastics. These will outgas over time onto the photos. Don't use items that have polyvinyl-chloride (PVC) plastics. Use plastics that are specifically labeled safe for archival storage and photo use. Safe plastic products are made with polypropylene or polyethylene.

- Consider extreme compression. The pressure of weight and gravity is not good for photos. Store your photos in an upright, vertical position. Do not stack them lying flat.

- Watch out for chemical reactions. Store photos separately from negatives. Not only is this a good idea in case of a disaster, it keeps the varied chemicals from interacting between the two mediums. Wooden boxes or containers like wooden baskets are not good for storage of photos. Do not store photos in rooms with a lot of chemical interchange, such as kitchens, garages, shops or laundry rooms.

- Hands carry body salt, oil and dirt that cannot be seen or detected. These contaminants transfer to the photos with handling. Wash hands before working with photographs. Wipe the photo with a clean, nonabrasive cotton cloth after you handle it. After scrapbooking, wipe the page gently when you finish it to decrease this risk. There are also hand lotions developed to neutralize hand oils. Some scrapbookers wear gloves while handling photos and scrapbooking. Use page protectors available for your album style. Decrease handling risks whenever possible.

- Keep your photos away from bright light and sunlight. Continuous light fades photos. Rotate photos that are hung on walls so that no one photo is exposed to direct light more than one year. Keep photos out of ultraviolet light as much as possible, including black lights.

ORGANIZATION

Sort your photos chronologically regardless of how you plan to scrapbook them later. If you can find the photo, you can pull it out later for specialty albums or emotion and sentiment pages. Our minds think chronologically. When you think of a photo, you naturally recall when it was taken. You remember how old the child was, or when the vacation was, in the context of your personal history. Use that personal chronological timeline as a basis for your photo filing system.

WHAT YOU'LL NEED

- 4 x 6" index cards in several colors OR the photo work sheet on page 41

- One or more large photo storage boxes

- Black journaling pen

- Negative holders if sorting negatives (see page 42) at the same time as you sort photos

- Page protectors or a large box if sorting memorabilia (see page 44) at the same time as you sort photos

- Time and table or floor space to work on this project over the course of a few days

- All of your loose photos (and negatives and memorabilia)

- Sticky notes for journaling

- Any calendars you have saved to help identify photo dates and events

ORGANIZATIONAL HOW-TO

Gather up all the photos from around the house. Bring them into one room. Make a work sheet or an index card for each year. You may also make cards for each event if you have enough photos to warrant it. Later, sort by month. Finally, sort by event, if needed. While sorting, jot down memories the photos trigger involving events and people in the photos. If you are unsure when the event in a photo took place, estimate the time frame based on clues in the photo. Ages of children, hairstyles, cars, skirt lengths, hats, shoes and clothing styles all help pinpoint various eras. File these photos and their negatives in a separate container to investigate at a later time. Storing photos in chronological order will now be easy. Use photo storage boxes, files, or slip-in-sleeve type albums to store photos by date until you are ready to scrapbook.

STORAGE

Photo storage options abound. How you store your priceless pictures will depend on how often you want to view them, how much work you want to go through to showcase them, and how many of them you have to work with. Do you want all your photos in scrapbooks? Or do you feel the majority can go into sleeve albums or boxes while saving the scrapbooking for the most special photos? Regardless of what you choose for storage, keep in mind that photos are best stored at 60-75 degrees Fahrenheit for optimal longevity.

Before you file your organized photos and memorabilia away in chronological order, be sure to jot down pertinent information on index cards or a photo work sheet for future reference when scrapbooking. Tag or mark any accompanying memorabilia for future scrapbooking as well.

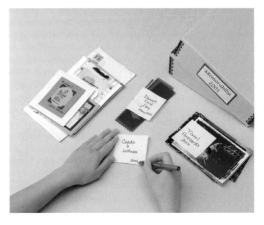

PLASTIC BOXES & TOTES

These are often called photo supply boxes or photo totes. These come in varying sizes and styles. Sort your photos first to determine the number and size you need. Plastic boxes should be made from polypropylene, acrylic or polyethylene. Some fit under the bed and have handles and rollers. New research suggests that wooden boxes may not be best for long term photo storage. Even treated wood contains acid and lignin which can release gas over time. Choose an alternative to wood if possible.

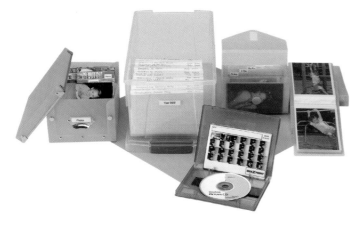
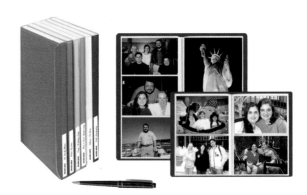

Among the popular, archival-plastic photo storage containers are (left to right): Kokuyo's large E-Z Snap storage boxes, Rubbermaid's photo and media storage boxes, and un-du's PhotoKeeper™, which can hold photos, negatives and a CD-ROM. For transporting sets of photos to crops for scrapbooking, try Generations' Foto Friend™ accordion wallet with Velcro® fastener or Kokuyo's photo storage albums with sleeve cases. To store photos and negatives until you can scrapbook, try Pioneer's Space Saver™ albums with cases (above right) or Leeco/Cropper Hopper's Photo Case (right).

Acid-free, archival-safe cardboard photo storage can be an inexpensive but effective way to store photos. Some of today's popular choices are (left to right): Generations/K & Co.'s Photo Express, Pioneer's Photo Box, Highsmith's Photo Chest and Photo Keepers, and Colorbök's the Perfect Scrapbook™ Memory Storage box and photo folders. Try Jotter's Pocket Jotter™ for noting memories about photos before storing them.

ACID-FREE CARDBOARD BOXES & KEEPERS

These are most often made for 4 x 6" photos or smaller, but there are some available for enlargements and panoramic photos. Certain cardboard photo storage containers come with dividers, or you can use index cards to label the years. Other units have drawers to accommodate decades of photos, while still others have handles for portability.

RECYCLE PHOTO DUPLICATES

Sort and label duplicate photos and then let a family member store them for you in an archival photo storage box. This will ensure that if natural disaster strikes your home, you will have photos elsewhere. Duplicates that you no longer care about may be given to family members or friends. Or consider using them to make a "year in review" scrapbook page spread—or a calendar, greeting cards or gift tags.

If you save photo scraps to crop and use as page accents, sort them by color regardless of theme, and store in an accordion-style plastic folder such as Caren's Crafts' Scrap-N-File™ mini accordion file, which has elastic bands to keep photo scraps snug and organized.

Polaroids

Polaroids need basically the same care as regularly developed photos with a few added elements.

• The main hazard of Polaroid prints is before they are fully developed. Handle all parts with care. The processing jelly, which contains sodium hydroxide or potassium hydroxide, can be highly caustic. It remains at a high pH on the discarded portion (the non-image and negative area) for up to two hours. It is highly corrosive to the skin, eyes and mucous membranes. Avoid skin or eye contact with residual processing fluid. If children chew or ingest film, flush with water and contact a poison control center.

• Dispose of wet negatives in a closed waste container to prevent further contact.

• Leave Polaroid "integral" prints intact. An integral print, noted for its thickness and ¾" lower white border, contains chemicals that can leak out when the edges are cut open. Peel-apart prints are safe to cut because the chemical-containing negative is separated from the positive print.

• Do not use adhesives on Polaroids. The chemicals in the glues may react with the backing and chemicals of the photograph. A safer storage solution for Polaroids is to use large photo corners to hold the photo in place on a scrapbook page. You may also place photos in plastic memorabilia sleeves or pockets.

Advantix

• Store unexposed film and disposable cameras at 70 degrees Fahrenheit or cooler. Always store film (exposed or unexposed) canisters in a cool, dry place.

• Process film as soon as possible after exposure.

• Advantix negatives never leave their canisters. Special organizer boxes can be purchased for holding these negatives that look like film canisters.

• Do not disassemble the Advantix negative cassette. Store the cassette in a cool, dry place with its index print. Label both for ease in later identification.

Pioneer's Advanced Photo Case™ and Advanced Photo Storage Box™ provide the perfect archiving environment for Kodak's Advantix™ film and corresponding index prints.

Slides

- Archival slide holder sheets are available that hold up to 20 slides. These are then labeled and stored in notebook binders by subject or by date. These slide sheets can also be hung from hanging file slide rods and stored in file cabinets.

- Good labeling is key. Ensure that you can find what you want by labeling accurately. Create an index sheet that lists the slides' topics and dates; store chronologically or by theme.

- Do not store slides in daylight conditions. Cases for storage binders are available or store the slides in the slide reels in which they came inside an acid-free box. Or store them in the semi dark of the file cabinet as hanging files. Keep in mind that the original slide reel boxes are probably not archival.

- Sturdy slide storage boxes are available from photo supply houses. These can hold up to 200 slides each. Label and store at a moderate temperature around 75 degrees Fahrenheit.

Try Kokuyo's Color 'N' Color Collection three-ring binders, outfitted with Pioneer's archival-quality slide protector sleeves and an index sheet, to organize and store slides.

Audio- & videotapes

With the advent of the camcorder, family videos abound. Learn to care for your family videos so they last as long as possible. The shelf life of family camcorder and homemade video movies is much shorter than originally thought. Consider having them transferred to longer-lasting DVDs.

- Keep recordings free of dirt, dust and mildew.

- Play as little as possible. Each playing depletes some of the quality and the lifetime of the recording.

- Videotapes last between 10 and 30 years. Treating cassettes and videotapes carefully should increase their life span.

- Handle cassettes and videotapes as little as possible. Never touch the tape section with your fingers.

- Avoid extreme heat and humidity.

- Play and rewind sound recordings and family videos as little as possible. Each time you rewind a tape it traps dust and debris between the layers, which can scratch the tape's surface and impede the quality of its playback.

- Do not smoke near your cassettes and videotapes.

- Avoid pausing your cassettes and videotapes too long or too often. Pausing stretches the tape.

- Keep all electronic and magnetic storage (like videos and floppy disks) away from magnets.

- Store in temperature-regulated areas of the home.

- Store cassettes and videotapes upright or on end.

- Do not store in the attic or garage where heat can be a great enemy of vinyl recordings, audiotape and videotape.

- Humidity is dangerous to audiotape. The tape actually absorbs the water from the air and degrades the recording.

- Video storage boxes and tubs are available to control dust and humidity.

Archival-quality storage boxes for videocassettes—such as Pioneer's lidded video storage boxes with index cards—can add life to these precious taped memories.

Work sheet for sorting photos

YEAR: _____

JANUARY	**JULY**
FEBRUARY	**AUGUST**
MARCH	**SEPTEMBER**
APRIL	**OCTOBER**
MAY	**NOVEMBER**
JUNE	**DECEMBER**

Source: Barbara Tolopilo, Family Treasures, Inc.

Negatives

The secret to preserving your treasured negatives is to handle them as little as possible. Place them in archival-safe containers or albums. Store these collections in the coolest environment in your home. Keep them away from large variations in temperature and humidity.

CARE

- Wash and dry your hands thoroughly before handling negatives. Keep your hands free of oils, body salts and moisture while handling negatives. Dust your work surface before laying down negatives.

- Wear cotton gloves when previewing negatives to prevent scratching. Hold the negatives on the outer edges only. This prevents smudging.

- Avoid cutting negative strips when organizing or reordering reprints. Cutting a negative ruins the emulsion, thus ruining the negative. Cutting negatives also means you have handled them again and added to the risk of fingerprinting or permanently scratching the small surface area.

- Clean dirty negatives with a negative-cleaning solution, such as PEC-12.

- Like your photos, keep your negatives away from dust, bright light, excessive heat and high humidity.

- Consider storing negatives "off site." In the event of a disaster, they'll be safe.

*Clean negatives, if needed, with Photographic Solutions' PEC-12® Emulsion Cleaner and PEC*PAD® Non-Abrasive Wipes. Handle clean negatives with Highsmith's lint-free cotton gloves to prevent skin oils from transferring.*

ORGANIZATION

As you sort the photos into safer environments, sort your negatives as well. Organize your negatives just as you do your photos. Sort them chronologically, by subject matter or by theme. It will be easier to understand a chronological-order system for those who inherit the negatives. Taking the time to sort negatives now translates into more efficient scrapbooking later on. The two basic storage systems for negatives that scrapbookers use with success are the binder or the box system.

BINDER SYSTEM: WHAT YOU'LL NEED

Binders are a convenient and economical way to organize and store negatives. For this type of negative storage system, you will need:

- Binder-style, three-ring notebook
- Archival negative sleeves
- Unsorted negatives

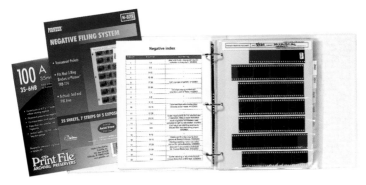

Store clean negatives in Pioneer's three-ring binder albums, outfitted with the company's Negative Filing System archival sleeves, a correlating index sheet, and notebook tab index dividers to separate months or years. Print File® is another quality company that manufactures archival, PVC-free negative preserver sleeves.

Keep the negatives in complete strips and in chronological order. Archival negative sleeves hold one strip of negatives per row. The sleeves should be labeled with date, event, and people in the photo. Be consistent in your labeling. Always put the full date on the negative sleeve where you can see it. Then add the event name and the person's name. If exact dates are not known, give your best estimate. Place the filled negative sleeves into a three-ring binder and create tabs for various months or years. Add an index sheet at the front of the binder with a listing of the photo events in that binder. Label each binder on the spine for quick reference.

BOX SYSTEM: WHAT YOU'LL NEED

Negatives may also be stored in boxes as long as the boxes are archivally safe and there are acid- and lignin-free strips of paper between the negatives to prevent sticking. You'll need:

• A negative storage box

• Acid- and lignin-free paper strips or negative pockets a little larger than the negatives

• An archival pen that will write well on paper or plastic

• Negatives that need sorting

Keep the negatives in complete strips and in chronological order. Negatives that are sliced into small sections are too easily lost or damaged and are hard to file. Label the strips of paper with data about the negative. Keep your writing on the white slip at the top of the paper so as not to affect the negative film filed in front of it. Be certain to add a strip of acid-free paper between negative strips to prevent them from sticking together. Label the box with full dates. Add an index sheet of dates and events related to each box of negatives.

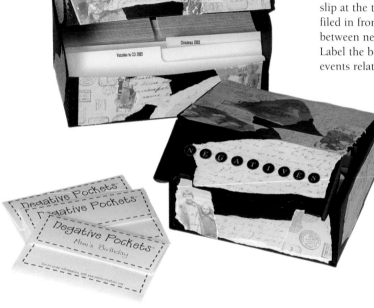

Some popular archival cardboard negative containers include Highsmith's Acid-Free Photo Tote and Acid-Free Negative Box, which can be decorated. Or, try Light Impressions' FoldLock™ negative sleeves stored inside their negative storage boxes. The Sentimental Playground manufactures acid- and lignin-free Negative Pockets™, which are a convenient way to organize and label your negatives once the companion photos have been put in albums.

STORAGE

• Use only 100% acid-free, lignin-free, and PVC-free negative sleeves, storage binders and storage boxes. Buy from reliable brands and sources.

• Store in a climate-controlled area. Avoid extremes in chemical vapors, lighting, heat and humidity.

• Store negatives in temperatures between 65-70 degrees with about 30 percent humidity. Humidity over 60 percent is harmful. Use anti-desiccant canisters or room dehumidifiers if necessary.

• The best place for negative storage is in a safe place out of your home such as a bank vault, safe-deposit box or with a family member. If natural disaster strikes, it is unlikely it will hit both homes at the same time.

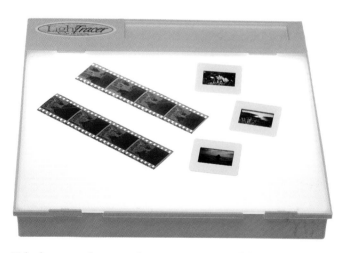

Make the process of sorting and organizing negatives and slides much faster by viewing them on Artograph's budget-friendly Light Tracer® light box.

Memorabilia

Memorabilia, also called "ephemera," are other treasured possessions that accumulate through the years. Memorabilia can include anything from lockets of hair and sports patches to brochures and newspaper clippings. With proper care, organization and storage, memorabilia can be easily accessible for scrapbooking.

CARE

As the family scrapbooker, it is up to you to treat these documents and memorabilia so that they will last as long as possible. Many of these documents—such as construction paper art and newspaper—tend to disintegrate quickly. Newspaper articles, school artwork and many other private documents are not created on acid-free papers or archivally safe products. Items like these need to be preserved for their genealogical and historic value as well as family sentiment. Try these handy preservation suggestions:

- Make second copies of irreplaceable documents by copying them onto acid-free, archival-safe paper stock. You can store or scrapbook the original and have a backup copy on a more stable type of paper. Consider photocopying historic documents on oatmeal-colored paper to preserve the antique look.

- Spray documents with an acid-neutralizing spray. Most family and legal documents are not created on archival papers. It is a good safety measure to spray them with an archival spray to stop the acidic decomposition.

- Store newspapers separately. Never store newsprint with other non-newsprint documents. The acidic nature of the newsprint may contaminate other documents. Place the newsprint in page protectors or memorabilia keepers after it has been treated with an archival spray.

For acid-free cardboard storage of memorabilia, try (left to right): Highsmith's Acid-Free Memory Boxes, Generations' Memory Express™, General Box Co's. Tower of Boxes, or for large artwork, maps, etc., Light Impressions' TrueCore™ Drop-Front Box. Decorate as desired to identify the type of memorabilia stored in each box.

- Store documents and memorabilia in a climate-controlled environment. Pick a cool, dark and dry place for the storage of these family treasures.

- Use acid-free, archival-safe materials to encapsulate questionable memorabilia before adding to a scrapbook. Polypropylene sheet protectors and memory keepers are useful for this purpose.

- If your item is too large or you have space limitations, consider photographing the items and getting rid of the original. This is a particularly good idea for 3-D school projects, sports trophies, band uniforms, military uniforms and bulky, homemade items of only slight sentimental value (see next page).

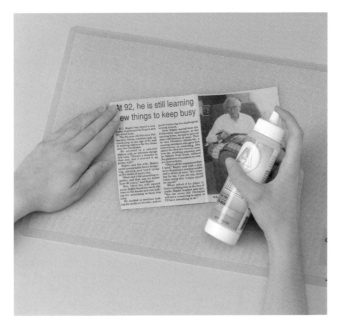

De-acidify memorabilia with a spray such as EK Success' Archival Mist® before adding it to a scrapbook page. An alternative to spraying is to photocopy the newsclipping or document onto acid-free paper.

ORGANIZATION

It is a good idea to sort and organize your memorabilia at the same time that you are sorting photos and negatives. This will make it easier to "match up" memorabilia with any corresponding photos when scrapbooking. Organize memorabilia by theme, such as home, military, baby, school, sports, etc., then organize it chronologically. Index what is in each box, page protector or pocket, and label accordingly. Label memorabilia by box or bag number. Be sure to note the number on your photo index cards or photo work sheet of any corresponding memorabilia so that you'll know where to find it. Keep your memorabilia files up-to-date. Make two copies of your index. One copy is for you to have as a reference. The other copy is to keep in/on the actual storage device as a content index. For example, glue one listing on the outside the storage box and put the other copy with your organized photos. You'll then be able to locate the items quickly by using the reference.

STORAGE

Common cardboard boxes are not a safe solution for document and memorabilia storage. Plastic boxes should be made from polypropylene, acrylic or polyethylene. Invest in a few high-quality archival boxes for your important family documents. Consider implementing one or a combination of these useful memorabilia storage options:

BAGS

Polyethylene bags of all sizes are available. Sort by date, type of event, theme or person. There are also specialty zipper-type bags for this purpose that are archivally safe.

BOXES

These are often called rare-book boxes or portfolio boxes. Memorabilia boxes can be purchased at scrapbooking and archival supply outlets. Dry cleaners often have access to acid-free boxes in larger sizes. More recently, some of the scrapbooking vendors have created under-the-bed models from safe plastics, cardboard and other materials.

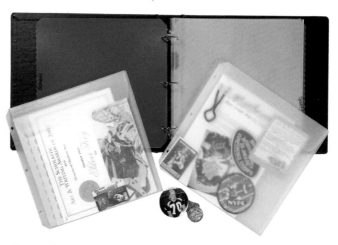

If you prefer storing organized memorabilia in binders, Generations' Memorabilia Pockets, separated by their Memory Album Dividers, work well in 12 x 12" binders or albums from Collected Memories.

ACCORDION FILES

Make sure these are acid-free and archival-safe. Ordinary cardboard office supply styles are generally not archival quality.

HANGING FILES

Set up a labeled folder for each year and file your memorabilia accordingly. Break it down by month if needed.

SCRAPBOOK ALBUMS

Scrapbooks come in sizes ranging up to 15 x 18" along with archival page protectors to fit. This size accommodates most larger items and documents.

THREE-RING BINDERS WITH PAGE PROTECTORS

These will store most small paper and flat mementos. Label the spines with the items and dates included.

Photographing memorabilia

- Outdoors, use 200-speed film and flash; shoot in open shade or soft sunlight.
- Indoors, use 400-speed film and flash; shoot in well-lit location or late in the day for a nostalgic effect.
- Arrange memorabilia on floor or tabletop in an eye-pleasing display.
- Fill the frame with your arrangement when you look through the camera's viewfinder.

- Get as close as possible to accurately record words and numbers.
- Snap many photos from different angles, rearranging memorabilia as needed for visual appeal.
- For a photography alternative for flat memorabilia such as ribbons and certificates, scan the item(s), either alone or in collage-style, reduce the size and print on acid-free paper of choice.

Computer Files & Digital Images

The Information Age has impacted scrapbooking in a big way, creating the need to care for, organize and store computer files and digital images. From font CDs, downloaded fonts and digital photographs to favorite Web site "bookmarks," computer files can quickly become hard to find because of sheer volume. The first rule when storing digital images and computer files is to back up your data. Make at least two copies and store them in different places. One copy can be on your hard drive but make sure another copy is elsewhere. You just never know when tragedy might strike! Use these tips to help you keep your computer files and digital images in tiptop shape.

Keep your CD-ROMs and floppy disks in tip-top shape by storing in jewel cases in a tower or in Light Impressions' Slimline CD Album with CD pages. For a collection of floppy disks, try Kokuyo's small E-Z Snap storage box.

Computer files

- Online storage is not recommended for exclusive or long-term storage of your images. However there are online services that will store your digital images for a monthly fee. Be warned that some of these companies have clauses that protect them from lawsuit should they go out of business and/or mistakenly delete your files! Be sure to back up any online photo storage with real prints or CDs.

- Hard drive storage of images is only recommended for very short-term storage until you can burn a CD of the image files.

- Upload items from the hard drive as soon as possible to photo processing sites and order prints or print them at home with archival ink and acid-free papers.

- Keep your hard drive folders sorted and be sure that the names accurately reflect the contents. Trash folders on a regular basis when you find that you never use them.

- Make it a point to regularly file and sort through your computer bookmarks. Many no longer function after six months. Create a subfolder within your "bookmark" or "favorites" folder and drag all scrapbooking-related Web sites to that folder.

- Use a font organizer program. Fonts can be addictive. They can also overload your system if you have too many. Weed through duplicates that can be deleted. Font organizers help you see which fonts need installing and what they look like. You can print out a hard copy to use as a reference.

CD-ROMs

- All photographic images can be scanned or converted to electronic images and stored on CD. You can make electronic slide shows or photo albums. This medium may not last forever but it is a good secondary storage device at the moment.

- Store your image master CDs "off site" in a safe-deposit box as you would negatives.

- Keep the temperature normal and humidity low. According to a major CD manufacturer, writable CDs will have a data lifetime of greater than 200 years if stored in the dark at 60 degrees Fahrenheit and 40 percent relative humidity. When stored in a 70-degree Fahrenheit home environment, the lifetime of a writable CD should be at least 100 years or more.

- Even though CDs normally have a long shelf life, they can be damaged. Do not drop, scratch, warp or heat a CD.

Digital images

- Store your digital data in more than one place, more than one copy and more than one format. Make a hard copy if possible for anything irreplaceable in your digital files like heritage photos, genealogy documents or family portraits.

- Regularly upload your camera to your hard drive and save your images on the hard drive to a writable CD. Do this at least monthly.

- Use a folder system to organize the computer storage of images.

- Sort photo uploads by date but also add something in the folder title that describes the event or subject. Example: 2/03/01 Nana Jones' birthday party and gifts.

- Make a date with your computer. Regularly upload images to photo sites and have them printed or print them yourself.

- Once a CD has several months' worth of photos on it, take it in to be developed at a photo center. Many photo centers develop directly from the CD.

- A CD can store up to 700 MB. Just a handful of CDs can store your entire photo collection. Just make sure they are in folders and labeled with, at minimum, the chronological dates.

If you work faster on a computer than you do manually, you may find that software programs for scrapbooking organization are just what you need. Try LNS Software Solutions' Organized Expressions™ for Scrapbooking (for MS Windows) or Handango's MyCraftCompanion by C. Cirelli Palm-Pilot®-style organizer shareware.

Scrapbooking software

Digital scrapbook gurus will be happy to know that there is an organizing software—Organized Expressions™ for Scrapbooking —available from LNS Software Solutions. The MS Windows™-based program allows you to keep track of your supplies, swaps, page-layout ideas and more. For Palm-Pilot® users, there's Handango's MyCraftCompanion by C. Cirelli—a shareware organizer program. It allows you to track supplies, page submissions, entry deadlines, swaps and more even when you're on-the-go. Even if you don't create digital scrapbook pages, these user-friendly software programs can help you get organized.

Top eight good reasons to do a backup

Power surges

A sudden oversupply of electric power can damage the files on your hard drive.

Hard drive crashes

Your files can be lost due to a network system or electrical failure.

Human error

You accidentally drop the hard drive, delete a file or reformat a disk.

Hackers

Someone could tamper with the information on your computer.

Theft

Someone can copy or delete information from your computer or steal the entire unit.

Natural disasters

A natural disaster could destroy your computer and hard drive.

Magnetic interference

Your floppy disk could come in contact with magnetic material, erasing files.

Electronic viruses

Your hard drive or disks could become infected, compromising their data.

Non-Consumable Tools & Supplies

What is a hobby without tools? Non-consumable tools and supplies are those that keep on giving and giving until they eventually break or wear out. Your tools are some of the most important aids to creativity during the page-making process. Misplacing a tool, breakage and duplicate purchases can all add to the chaos of an unorganized workspace. This can be avoided if you know what you have, where it is located and how to care for it. Gather up all your tool supplies from around the house. Check the totes, bins, bags and even the car! Sort tools by type. Keep like items together. Get rid of any tool that you never intend to use (see pages 34-35). Once you've weeded out the chaff, clean and label supplies and determine what kind of containers you will need to store them. Transparent and labeled containers and bins, and notebooks with labeled dividers can make it faster to locate the items you need.

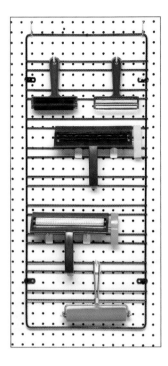

Brayers & crimpers

- Keep your crimpers and brayers as clean and dust free as possible. Serious dust buildup can cause roller jams.

- Keep fingers out of the way of the rolling bar on brayers and crimpers.

- These types of tools are generally used less frequently than others. Store labeled in a clear, lidded bin, in the drawer of a cart or on hooks on pegboard.

- Crimpers, brayers and other "T-shaped" tools can also be stored on hangers or stands designed for paint rollers and rakes.

Brayers and crimpers are happy hung on Sturdi-Craft's pegboard and pegboard hooks. Pegboard on a wall is a great solution for hanging tools that aren't used as often as others.

Create an inventory notebook

While dividing, conquering, cleaning and labeling your tools and supplies, make a tool inventory in a scrapbook inventory notebook. These are sold commercially (see left) or you can make your own. A scrapbook inventory notebook allows you to keep track of what you own in each tool category. Don't buy duplicates ever again!

- Get a notebook or binder in a size you like. If you plan to take it shopping, it should be a small planner size of binder with plenty of blank pages.

- Make a full listing of each tool category. Include details such as the names of decorative scissor blades, pen colors and brands, and letter template font names and sizes. The more tool details you include the better.

- Keep in mind that papers such as cardstock and printed pattern papers do not need to be inventoried because they get used so quickly. Creating an inventory of all your papers would be time-consuming and nearly impossible to keep up to date. Instead, inventory your more permanent, non-consumable items like the tools featured on the following pages.

- Take your notebook shopping. You will know for a fact whether you have a particular decorative scissor, die, punch or stamp.

Artfully Scribed's Scrap-A-Log™ is a handy little notebook that comes with preprinted pages for cataloging your tools and supplies. The log also helps keep track of page layout ideas, web sites, store information, publications and wish lists.

Craft knives

- Keep them sharp; replace the blades often.

- Use an emery board to sharpen larger blades periodically.

- Clean blades with rubbing alcohol or un-du® to remove any adhesive residue. Dry thoroughly.

- Store out of the reach of children.

- Store blades inside of protective sheaths.

- Always store your knives in the same easy-access location. This is one often-used tool you don't need surprising you later if misplaced in the wrong bin, drawer or caddy.

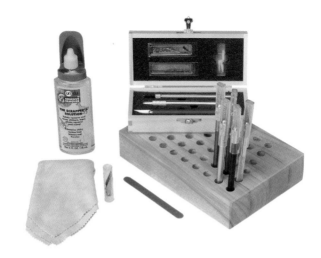

Armada Art's solid oak blocks provide a great little home for craft knives or scissors if you prefer desktop storage. Hunt Corporation's X-ACTO knives come in their own utility case. Use un-du's adhesive remover to clean knives and sharpen with an ordinary nail file or sharpening stone or replace with new blades.

Shape croppers and mat cutters generally store well in lidded containers, such as this Rubbermaid® unit, to keep them dust-free. If you keep your paper trimmer on your desktop, dust occasionally with a soft towel or feather duster. Replace blades as necessary.

Croppers & cutters

- Cropping tools like shape cutters need fresh blades regularly. If you try to save a few pennies on a new blade but end up ruining a photo with a dull cutter, where are the savings?

- Clean blades and bodies with alcohol or un-du® to remove any residue. Dry thoroughly.

- Store out of the reach of children.

- Cutters and blades should be stored in tightly closed containers for safety.

- If you use your paper trimmer frequently, tuck it out of view from children when you are not scrapbooking.

Dies & die-cut machines

- Remove any paper bits, particles or dust from dies and machines, using tweezers if needed to get into tiny crevices.

- Organize dies alphabetically or by theme, depending upon the size of your collection.

- Store dies in commercially made wooden-box racks or corrugated storage compartments, specialty binders from the manufacturer or specially made spinning racks.

- Die-cut machines can be bulky and heavy. If you don't use the machine daily, store it away from tiny fingers.

Store standard-sized dies in Accu-Cut's laminate towers (available in many sizes) or for smaller dies, try Sizzix/Provo Craft's Die Storage System. Store QuiKutz' dies in the company's EZ-Store Sheets and Storage Binder.

Miscellaneous tools

Many scrapbook tools have metal and movable parts. Care should be taken to maintain the metal so it remains in prime condition. Because these tools are used quite frequently while scrapbooking, you'll want to keep them handy—preferably on the desktop. Good care will maintain the lever action of movable parts. Proper care and storage will give you years of use for these kinds of tools: metal straightedge and graphing rulers, hammer, eyelet setter, tweezers, piercing tool, embossing stylus, button-shank remover, round needle-nose pliers and scissors. Keep tools and their handles dry, dust free and clean of adhesives and colorant residue. Store in a desktop caddy, tool box or in handled totes or zippered bags for cropping on-the-go.

Convenient desktop tool caddies include The Pampered Chef's Tool Turnabout, Westwater Enterprises' Canvas Craft Caddy, Armada Art's Small Art Supply Caddy, Inventor's Studio's Fold 'N Hold's mesh caddy, Twin Ray's Organize-Up clamp-on Craft Space Organizer or ArtBin's Solution Boxes.

Punches

- Punches should be kept dry and out of humidity to prevent rusting.

- Remove jammed paper from the punch with tweezers. If that doesn't work, place punch in the freezer for 20 seconds. The metal will contract for easy paper removal.

- Temperatures below 32 degrees Fahrenheit may be harmful to the plastic casings. Repeated cold temperatures make plastics brittle before their time. Try not to let your punches freeze. Do not leave them in the car overnight if you live in a cold climate.

- When dull, punch through heavy-duty aluminum foil.

- When a punch sticks, punch through wax paper several times to re-lubricate.

Dull and sticking punches can be sharpened and lubricated with heavy-duty aluminum foil and wax paper. Create a quick reference guide by filling a small notebook with each punched shape from your collection. Organize pages by size, type or theme.

- Use un-du® to clean off adhesive residue left by stickers, tape and self-adhesive paper. Simply squirt the solution on the underside of the punch. Punch through scrap paper until all of the solvent has evaporated.

- Keep track of which punches you own. Punch a sample from black paper and mount it onto white cardstock sheets. Label each with name, size and brand. Add this reference to a scrapbook inventory notebook (see page 48).

- Store punches in a dry place and protect against moisture and dust. Clear containers have the added advantage of

visibility. If possible, label your storage containers in the same manner that you label your punch reference guide.

- Store in over-the-door pocket organizers, bins, toolboxes or plastic drawer units. For cropping-on-the-go, take punches in special totes, bags and carryalls made specifically for this purpose.

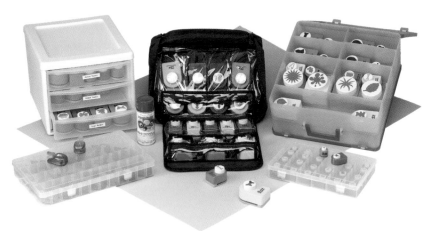

Punch storage comes in a wide array of sizes and styles. Try storing punches in ArtBin's Clear View boxes, Sterilite's drawer towers, McGill's Punch 'N Go tote or Leeco/Cropper Hopper's Supply Case. Tutto offers a Punch & Stamp Holder™ carrying tote and Crop In Style® provides an over-the-door Punch Pal™ that can grow as your punch collection grows.

Scissors

- Clean all metal blades, both regular and decorative, with adhesive remover after you cut through adhesive-backed papers.

- Decorative scissors are hard to sharpen professionally. Cut through heavy-duty aluminum foil to bring back their edge.

- Straightedge scissors can be sharpened professionally at any hardware or fabric store. Or you can do it yourself with a sharpening stone. Hand-held stones are often sold in the scissor section of fabric stores.

- Add a drop of lubricating liquid when scissor levers get stiff. Wipe well with a clean cloth before using on paper.

- Store scissors either horizontally in bins or drawers or hanging with the tips downward.

- Store out of the reach of children.

Scissor storing solutions include Tutto's scissor holder tote and Plaid's Creative Gear™ scissor holder tote. Crop In Style® makes the tri-fold Scissor Caddy. Armada Arts' Paper Shapers™ come in their own solid oak stand and Novelcrafts offers a triangular spinning rack for scissor storage.

Stamps

- Clean rubber stamps after every use. Use warm soapy water or a commercial stamp cleaner and a sponge or small tray and flat rubber scrubber.

- Dry completely with a lint-free cloth to avoid mildew on the rubber. Blot stamps gently on towel instead of rubbing them.

- If you have a large stamp collection, sort and organize stamps by design theme or style, artist, brand or alphabetically.

- Keep inventory pages or index cards in a notebook of all the stamps you own for quick identification and to avoid duplicate purchases. Rubber stamp each image on paper and sort the pages by theme.

- Store stamps in stamp travel cases or totes or in commercially manufactured stamp storage units made of wood or corrugated cardboard.

- Store rubber side down so you can see the image on the handle. Do not stack rubber stamps.

- Unmounted stamps can be stored in 3 x 5" or 4 x 6" slip-in-style, photo-sleeve page refills. File these pages by theme or by manufacturer in a three-ring binder. Unmounted stamps can also be stored in CD-ROM jewel cases.

Stampin' Up! offers Stampin' Scrub and Stampin' Mist Cleaner pads and refills to help keep stamps clean. The company also makes Powder Pals™ trays and brushes to assist in embossing powder recovery.

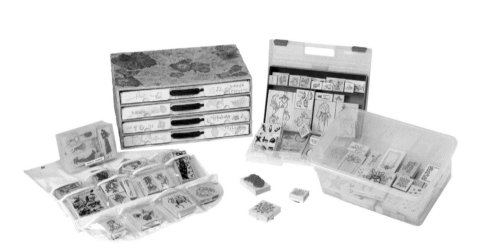

Keep stamps ready for use with Traffic Works' plastic boxes for smaller stamp collections, Highsmith's Stamp Storage Chest & Totes, Eagle Affiliates' Stamp Case, Rubbermaid's wide array of bins or Westwater Enterprises' Craft Pockets.

Crop In Style's Punch Pal™ (above) works nicely for stamps as well, and the company's stackable Stamp Store storage trays work great for stamping on-the-go. Try ArtBin's clear Prism™ boxes or Quick View carrying cases for stamping on-the-go with smaller stamp collections.

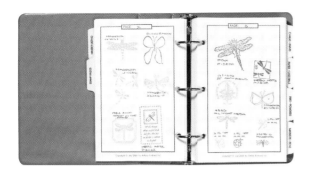

Artfully Scribed's Stamp-A-Log™ provides ultimate rubber stamp inventory organization in a three-ring binder format.

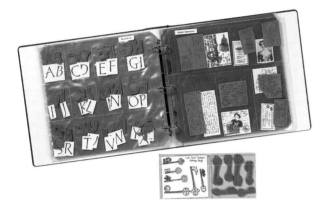

For unmounted stamps, try storing them in a Collected Memories album outfitted with C-Line Products' Memory Book® Page Protectors, Generations' Memory Album Dividers and the stamped image on paper. You can also store smaller unmounted stamp collections in CD jewel cases with the image stamped on scrap paper.

Templates & decorative rulers

- Wash plastic templates and rulers with warm soapy water and pat dry with cotton or paper toweling. Wash brass templates and stencils with plain warm water. Do not use soap unless you need to do so. Soap may discolor the brass and accelerate tarnishing. Dry thoroughly with cotton or paper toweling.

- Wipe off all templates and rulers with paper towels after each shape or letter is traced. It takes a minute or less for some inks to dry so wipe frequently.

- Remedy swivel-knife nicks in the plastic of graduated or "nested" templates as soon as you can. Many can be sanded horizontally using slight pressure with a fine emery board.

- Organize templates, stencils and decorative rulers into one of these categories: envelopes; tags and windows; frames; geometric shapes; letters; page-makers; puzzles; theme designs and decorative motifs. If desired, you can subdivide designs and motifs into holidays, seasonal, sport, travel, etc.

- Store all of your stencils, templates and embossing patterns in a three-ring binder, preferably a 12 x 12" binder so that all of your templates and stencils will fit together. If desired, insert templates into 12 x 12" page protectors or just insert them into the binder using the three holes punched into them. Label notebook dividers with the above categories.

- Insert a plain white paper between templates to prevent snagging and bending. Trace the template or stencil image onto the paper so you know which ones go where after each use.

- Smaller templates and stencils can be tucked into page protectors in the same binder.

- Brass templates and tiny stencils can be placed into baseball-card sleeves or mini photo albums for easy viewing and storage.

- Store binders flat.

For quick and easy template, stencil and ruler identification, try these handy storage products: Kokuyo's photo albums with cases or Crop In Style's Binder Buddy™ with the company's page refills and binder dividers. For Coluzzle™ Nested Templates, Provo Craft offers its own organizer tote.

TAKING STOCK II: CONSUMABLE TOOLS & SUPPLIES

With your physical workspace now in order, those chaotic scrapbook supply piles should be shrinking a bit. Your tools are organized and your photos, negatives and memorabilia are sorted. Now tackle the rest of your scrapbooking stash. Get started gathering, sorting, purging, labeling and storing those consumable supplies by type. For easy retrieval, keep like items with like items.

Goods such as albums, adhesives, embellishments, fibers, paper, pens and stickers are all items that come and go as you use them up. Storage for these should be flexible and have the ability to grow and shrink as your supplies regularly grow and shrink. Weed out consumables that you don't like. Keeping items you do not care to use takes up space and mental energy every time you must look for "the good stuff."

Keep in mind that what is trendy in scrapbooking today may not be in fashion next year. Keep only what you will love and will honestly use, and then tailor your storage to suit your personal needs. By whittling these types of supplies down to the essential "keepers," you will be able to scrapbook more rapidly and with less guilt and less debate. Every supply you keep should be a joy to use.

Consumable Tools & Supplies

In addition to non-consumable tools and supplies, the hobby of scrapbooking also brings with it consumable tools and supplies. Consumable supplies are those products that will have to be replenished over the course of time. Consumable supplies include adhesives, albums, cleaners, colorants, embellishments, sources of inspiration, paper and pre-made page additions—which include die cuts and stickers. Retail scrapbook and hobby stores are filled with aisles and aisles of these mesmerizing products. We buy all of the "gotta have 'em" items that we can afford. At home, we plunk the shopping bags down wherever there's room, only to paw through them and rediscover the items later while looking for something else. So now it's time to gather up all of your consumable tool and supplies from around the house. Sort and group the items, keeping like items together. Weed out those items that you're fairly certain you'll never use and get rid of them (see pages 34-35). Once you've determined all of the "keepers," decide what kind of containers you really need. Containers that will comfortably hold your current collections, plus a little room for growth, are ideal. Transparent and labeled containers and bins and notebooks with labeled dividers will make it easier to find just what you need.

Adhesives

Scrapbookers have access to a wide range of glues and tapes that make it quick and easy to attach photos, memorabilia, accents and embellishments to pages. Select only products that are acid-free and photo safe. Start by dividing your adhesives into two categories: wet and dry.

- Always put the cap back on wet adhesives; they dry out very quickly.

- Use a pin or piercing tool to unclog the spouts of bottled adhesives; wipe around tip with a damp cloth to keep clean.

- If you end up with adhesive where you don't want it, use adhesive remover or a white eraser to remove the surplus.

- Check wet adhesives every two months to see if they are still fluid and usable.

- Store dry adhesives in their original packages when not in use to prevent unraveling or sticking to other items.

- Buy tape runner cartridge refills as needed to avoid the cost of purchasing an entire new tape dispenser.

- A convenient time to remove residue from an adhesive application machine such as a Xyron™ is when you're changing adhesive cartridges. Use adhesive remover and a cotton swab to wipe residue away. Use a dampened cloth to wipe grime from the unit's body.

- Store all adhesives away from heat sources and out of sunlight.

Store sorted adhesives in rapid-access containers such as Rubbermaid's Slim Drawer or Quantum™ Storage Systems' 4-Drawer Tilt Bin or Stackable or Hangable bins. Keep your Xyron™ machine clean by removing any sticky residue with an adhesive remover and keep hands clean with un-du' s Acid Neutralizing Wipes.

Albums

Photo albums should be acid- and lignin-free, and the page protectors in them should be made of polypropylene or polyethylene plastics. Spine choices should also be considered for longevity. For example, steel closures always last longer than simple adhesive or sewn fiber bindings. In addition:

- Albums range in size from 5 x 7" up to 12 x 15". Shelves or bookcases should be deep enough so that the albums do not hang over the edge. This avoids needless bumping and tipping.

- Store upright on a shelf, leaving a tiny bit of "breathing room" between albums. Excessive compression of albums will crush photos and page accents over time.

- Do not store albums long term in a horizontal manner. Papers and photos will be crushed and compressed over time.

- Use a lightly dampened cloth to wipe excess grime from fabric and vinyl covers. Use a clear dust jacket to protect the album's cover from hand oils, dust and pollutants.

- Ideal storage conditions are the same as those for photos.

- If storing albums on open shelving, avoid sunlight and keep albums as dust-free as possible. Large computer monitor dust covers, available at office supply stores, can cover multiple albums.

- Spines should be labeled and facing outward so you can read them.

- Avoid the use of magnetic photo albums with static, liftable sleeves. They may be labeled "archival," yet these have been shown to be hazardous to photos.

Make it a point to remove photos from magnetic albums during your "getting organized" project. Remove photos by slipping a slender knife or dental floss beneath a corner to lift. If photos are firmly stuck, try using un-du's PhotoCare™ Solution. If the album's plastic overlay is stuck to your photos, consult a conservator. Never force a photo from a page. If photos have already begun to deteriorate, consider investing in reprints rather than attempting to remove. Never use heat to loosen photos.

Store albums upright on open shelving or in bookcases that are deep enough to accommodate the albums' width. Avoid packing the albums tightly together; excessive compression can damage pages and bindings over time. These beautiful 12 x 12" albums are from Colorbök.

To keep album covers dust-free, try Crop In Style's Protective Album Covers—available in 12 x 12" or 8½ x 11".

Keep albums dust-free with Highsmith's acid-free cardboard Album Cases. You can decorate the album case to identify the album type, if desired.

Cleaners

Cleaners, sprays and solvents need special care, particularly if there are small children in the home. If possible, keep cleaners in a locked toolbox for safety's sake. More helpful tips:

- Keep caps on tightly when products are not in use. Some cleaners evaporate rapidly and fumes can be overwhelming.

- Do not mix chemicals. Allow time for complete drying between chemical processes such as spraying with an archival fixative, using un-du® or inks, heat embossing, or applying liquid lacquers.

- Be careful with cleaners, sprays and solvents near a heat embossing gun. Do not use flamable archival sprays, adhesive remover or spray fixatives in the same room and at the same time as a heat gun. Read all label cautions when using these products indoors.

If possible, keep cleaners in a locked toolbox for safety's sake. Read all label cautions and warnings to be on the safe side, especially when using these products indoors.

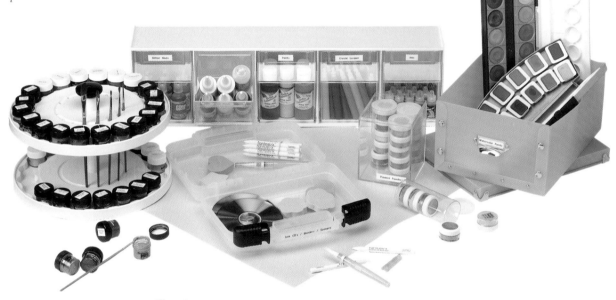

There are many good products available for storing enamels, lacquers and paints. Try Paintier Products' Paintier 40 Carousel, Quantum Storage System's 5-Drawer Tilt Bin or Kokuyo's large E-Z Snap storage box. Store sponges, water brushes, water pens and extra CD "palettes" in ArtBin's Quick View Carrying Case. Flex Products' Flexinizers™—available in many shapes and sizes—work great for stacking pearl powder pigments.

Colorants

Colorants are increasingly finding their way into our scrapbooks and overrunning our scrapbook workspaces. The selection of colorants for scrapbookers has expanded beyond basic pens, markers and ink pads to include chalks, paints and pigment powders, to name a few. Each colorant has its own distinct characteristics and unique properties, which impacts its own care and organization needs. These ideas should help you tame your coloring tools and supplies.

ENAMELS, LACQUERS & PAINTS

Paints are a dynamic medium that come in a spectrum of radiant colors and for different uses. Keep them in ready-to-use condition by following these guidelines:

- Keep watercolor paint palettes in good condition by mixing different paints on an old CD rather than on the paint palette.

- Add a few drops of water to pearl pigment powders on a CD to mix the medium. Do not mix the pigment powders and water in the original container. You are not likely to use all of this type of colorant in one sitting and premature mixing will only waste it.

- Pearl pigment paints never dry on plastic. You may store them in plastic however.

- Store acrylic and stencil paints right side up. Use within a year.

- Keep paintbrushes clean and store carefully to prevent damage to brush tips.

- If you use sponges to apply paint, be sure to wash them out with warm, soapy water and allow to air dry up to 48 hours before storing in a closed container.

- Close clear and crystal color lacquers tightly after use. Even a little air flow will dry the liquid. Use a sewing needle to unclog the lid dispensers of lacquer bottles.

- Store lacquers upright in their jars. This reduces dehydration and decreases leaks.

- Lacquers dry to a shiny, watery effect. Tap applied lacquer to see if it is dry after 24 hours before storing a scrapbook page. If it is firm, it is dry. Store lacquers upright and use within two years.

- Wipe the nozzles of glitter glues and glitter paints with a damp rag before capping. Unclog nozzles with a sewing needle or pin.

- Store enamels, lacquers and paints in their original containers.

- Organize enamels, lacquers and paints by grouping together by brand, type, color or frequency of use.

- Jars can be stored on a spinning rack made to hold small bottles or in bins, totes or drawers.

For large collections of jewel, acrylic or stencil paints, try Canvas Collectibles' over-the-door or wall mounted creative storage solution.

Store clean paintbrushes in ArtBin's Essentials Brush Box or Tutto's Brush Holder tote.

Here's just one of ArtBin's Quick View carrying cases. The company manufacturers a wide array of storage solution boxes and totes are perfect for colorants and other scrapbook tools and supplies.

EMBOSSING POWDERS & ENAMELS

Embossing powders, used primarily with stamping inks and embossing pens, come in a dazzling array of colors and textures, such as "ultra thick," pearl, tinsel and foil. Get the most out of your investment with these tips:

- Seal tightly after use.

- Sprinkle powders onto your art and catch any excess with a sheet of paper or recovery tray. Pour excess powder back into jar to avoid wasting it.

- Beware of the fumes. When heated, embossing powders release fumes as they turn from a solid to a liquid state. Do not inhale fumes or allow them in your eyes.

- Organize embossing powders and enamels by manufacturer, color or type.

- Store away from heat, moisture and water.

- Store in original jars on spinning racks, in trays, in stamp caddies, in bins or drawers. Storing powders upside down will enable you to see the powder colors easier.

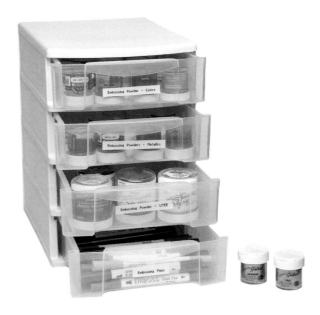

For ease in identification, sort embossing powders by type and then store upside down so that you can view the colors. Ours are stored in a Sterilite desktop drawer unit.

Whenever possible, store pencils in their original containers to be able to differentiate between standard and watercolor pencils. Organize by color grouping for quick access. For pencils that don't come in their own packaging, try storing in Armada Arts' Twist Tube or Kokuyo's small E-Z Snap storage box.

PENCILS

Probably the most under-utilized yet highly effective scrapbook colorant, pencils, are simple to care for, organize and store.

- Keep pencils dry, clean and sharpened.

- Do not drop. Lead is brittle and cracks easily.

- Organize pencils in rainbow-color groupings in original packaging, to be able to differentiate between ordinary color pencils and watercolor pencils.

- Water pens or brushes, used to wipe across watercolor pencils for a painterly effect, should be stored nearby for easy access.

- Store in pencil boxes, desk pen holders, flat-pack caddies or zippered pouches.

PENS FOR BLENDING

- While not a colorant, blender pens are used quite frequently to blend colorants. Keep close at hand for using to blend colorants.

- Before changing colors, wipe the blender tip clean on a scrap piece of paper.

- If the blender brush tip is frayed it can be replaced. Just pull the nib out and replace it with a new nib brush.

- Clean by wiping on clean paper or cloth.

- When your blender pen gets dry, pull the end cap off. Add several drops of blending fluid to refill.

PENS & MARKERS

Make sure your pens are the best possible choices for journaling and drawing in scrapbooks. Pens should be acid-free, fade- and waterproof pigment ink. In addition:

- Don't lose the caps. The minute you open a pen, you are in a race against evaporation. Keep caps on between uses.

- Use your pens regularly at least once a week. This keeps the ink flowing and the tips mobile.

- Avoid excessive writing on the backs of photos. Writing directly on photos may exert too much pressure on the back of the photo, creating visible indentations from the front.

- Many pens are not safe for writing on photo backs. If you want to write on your photos, do so in an inconspicuous place such as a corner. That way it will not affect the photo quality should the ink bleed through to the photo front.

- If you use a spray bulb to splatter ink from pen tips onto your scrapbook pages, immediately wipe the bulb tip with a damp cloth after each use to keep the tip color-free.

- Sort your pens regularly and toss out those that have dried out.

- Sort your pens by color, by type or by brand. Various types of pen points include calligraphy, brush, writer, scroll, bullet and chisel.

- Keep an inventory of what pens, tips, brands and colors you own to prevent duplication.

- While pen manufacturers vary in opinion on whether horizontal or vertical storage is best for pens, we recommend you store pens horizontally at least 90 percent of the time.

- Store pens upright in pen caddies or horizontally in shallow pen cases, boxes, bins or drawers.

- Store pens away from heat registers and drafts. Air movement speeds evaporation—even with the caps on!

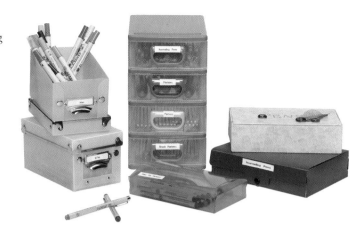

Pen storage options are many. Try Kokuyo's Kaddy™ supply tote (below) or small E-Z Snap storage boxes, Lion Products' Estima desktop drawer unit, General Box Company's Decorate Me™ boxes (we decorated ours!) or Traffic Works' wide array of plastic storage boxes.

For pen totes, try Plaid's Creative Gear™ Pen & Marker Holder or Tutto's Maker Holder tote. Crop In Style offers a 75-Pen Caddy, which stands up or folds flat (left). ArtBin's clear Prism™ and translucent Solutions™ boxes (below) have dividers for keeping pen types separate.

CHALK

Chalk—an inexpensive and popular scrapbook colorant because of its ease of use and versatility—needs special care.

- Keep chalks as dry as possible.

- Avoid dropping chalk cases; chalk palettes are fragile and break easily.

- Clear off extra dust from your chalks by blowing gently or rubbing the surfaces with cotton swabs.

- When using a chalk palette, do not press or twist your applicator into the chalk. Instead, sweep it lightly across the surface to keep chalk in good condition.

- Cover your work surface with paper towels before working withchalk.

- If you use a blender pen with chalks, use plain water so it will dry out evenly and not create an oily residue on top of your chalks.

- Keep a white eraser with your chalk. Chalk mistakes erase with ease.

- If you apply chalk with sponge-tip applicators, keep them clean with warm, soapy water. Allow to dry up to 48 hours before storing in a closed container.

- Spray chalked artwork with a fixative to prevent chalk particles from scattering.

- Store chalks in their original, compartmentalized containers inside zippered sandwich bags or in small supply cases with or without handles.

- Store gel metallic rub-ons closed. Wash all tools immediately after use to remove the fine colorant film.

INK PADS & INK DAUBERS

Make sure your ink pads are safe for your albums. Stamping inks and daubers should be acid-free, fade- and waterproof pigment ink. Available in rich and vibrant hues, ink pads and daubers last longer if you follow these tips:

- Make sure lids are on ink pads securely prior to storing.

- Ink pads should be stored horizontally. Some schools of thought believe that ink pads must be stored upside down.

- Use ink pads regularly to keep the ink sponges saturated.

- Dauber caps tend to fall off easily. Make sure they are secure to prevent dehydration.

- Sort and organize ink pads by color, ink types or brand names for easier identification.

- Ink refill bottles should be stored upright. Keep the caps on tightly.

- Store ink pads in special racks made of wood or corrugated cardboard made specifically for ink storage or in shallow bins, drawers, supply cases or totes.

Keep chalks and metallic rub-ons in their original palette containers. Store colorant applicators in Provo Craft's Bradletz Drawerz. Larger chalk palettes and rub-ons can be stored in Kokuyo's large E-Z Snap storage boxes. Store Craf-T's chalk enhancers and spray fixatives with cleaners, if possible.

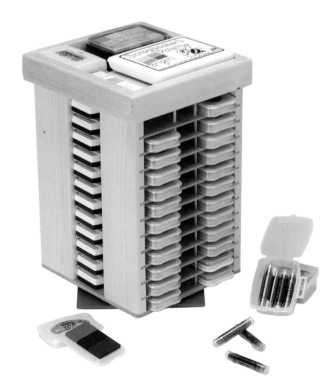

StampPadCaddy.com's Classic Caddy revolving carousel tower keeps ink pads organized and visible, with extra storage at the top for more pads. Tsukineko's ink daubers fit perfectly in TidyCrafts' rectangular Snappy Craft Containers. Other companies that make stamp pad storage include Last Dollar Designs and Port-a-Ink by CDJ Designs, LLC.

Embellishments

The boom in scrapbook embellishments has brought unique beauty and texture to pages along with a storage quandary for the scrapbook workspace. Because these items vary in size and bulk, it can be challenging to arrange them for easy access. How do you sort, organize and store all these baubles and trinkets? Don't fear! Solutions for taming all of your embellishments are right at hand.

METALLICS

Metal embellishments lend a shiny luster or masculine touch to scrapbooks. Metallics include bookplates, brad fasteners, charms, embossing metals, eyelets, frames, hinges, jewelry-making components, nailheads, photo corners, tags, wire, wire mesh, chains, penny nails and washers. Though tough and resilient by nature, metallics do require a little tender loving care where storage is concerned.

- Store all metal embellishments in low humidity. Flexible metals have alloys which can rust, as can those metals with iron in. (Test with a magnet. If a magnet can pick it up, it has iron in it.)

- Keep all metals dry and wiped free of hand oils which contain body salts. Salt, water, and other chemicals can lead to the corrosion of metal. Make sure you wipe all fingerprints and hand oils from metals before you encase them.

- Aluminum can oxidize, turning black over time. Make sure aluminum-coated or rimmed tags are not touching your photos.

- Copper oxidizes when exposed to air and gains a green patina or coating. This patina can flake off much. Keep copper items like tags, embellishments, copper eyelets and pennies encased and separated from your photos on the page.

- Label your eyelet hole punches with the size of hole it creates. Use a permanent marker to write S ($\frac{1}{16}$"), M ($\frac{1}{8}$"), and L ($\frac{1}{4}$") on the tip itself.

- Carry a sample of each eyelet color and size when you shop; to prevent buying duplicates. String one example of each color and style onto a large safety pin or a length of wire and tuck it in your handbag.

- Memorabilia keepers are great for encapsulating coins or heritage metal objects. This limits air flow, human contact and humidity changes.

- Sort such embellishments by type of item and then by color.

- Choose storage solutions that suit either your desktop, travel tote or both. Consider storage that effectively contains your organized embellishment collection, plus has a little room for growth to accommodate new items that attract your eye.

- Store in compartmentalized units, nut-and-bolt drawer organizers, watchmaker tins, compartmentalized trays, craft cases, a carousel outfitted with round containers made specially for craft supplies, stackable clear canisters, clear and flat compartment organizers and carrying cases with handles and tight-fitting lids.

For keeping metallic embellishments organized, try ScrapKings' aluminum cases with matching tins; Uniek's clear, round dispenser; Quantum Storage Products' 9-Drawer Tilt Bin; Provo Craft's Bradletz Drawerz; SCS/Hemline's compartmentalized Storage Organizer and Craft Storage Stackers, TidyCrafts' rectangular Snappy Craft Containers, and Making Memories' 18-compartment Sortables box and Stackables jar towers. For at-a-glance identification and shopping ease, add one type of each eyelet you own on a wire and twist ends to secure. And for a unique container that can mount under a desk or cabinet, try TidyCrafts' Eclipse™ container with six Shuttle Cups tucked inside (below).

BAUBLES

Baubles add an ornamental flair to scrapbook pages. These items include beads, buttons, confetti, gems, glitter, punched shapes, sequins, tiny glass marbles and more. All should have their own homes. These mini wonders add so much to your pages but are easily misplaced. To find what you need in a hurry:

- If the baubles are made of glass, stone or fired ceramic, they contain no acid and will not harm photos or scrapbooks.

- Plastic items are suitable as long as they do not contain PVC. If you're not sure whether a bauble is photo-safe, encapsulate it or place it away from photos.

- Remember that baubles are hard objects that can potentially scratch your photos; don't place photos opposite these items on a facing page.

- To avoid adding excess bulk to a page, use small and flat objects whenever possible.

- Sort such embellishments by type of item and then by color.

- Store in containers with clear bodies and/or lids that permit you to see what's inside, allowing for easier identification.

- Use containers that give your fingers easy access, close tightly and allow you to pour easily into a tray for further sorting.

- Choose storage solutions that suit either your desktop, travel tote or both. Consider storage that effectively contains your organized embellishment collection, plus has a little room for growth to accommodate new items that attract your eye.

- Store in compartmentalized units, nut-and-bolt drawer organizers, watchmaker tins, compartmentalized trays, craft cases, a carousel outfitted with round containers made specially for craft supplies, stackable clear canisters, clear and flat compartment organizers and carrying cases with handles and tight-fitting lids.

To contain baubles, try Eagle Affiliates' The Bead Tray, Flex Products' Flexanizers™, Magic Scraps' jar tower, TidyCrafts' round Pony Craft Containers, SCS/Hemline's round Craft Storage Stacker, Crop In Style's Itty-Bitty Box and Darice's The Ultimate Bead Box & Band. Beadalon's Mini Bead Tray works great for corralling and pouring tiny baubles.

TidyCrafts' Deluxe Carousel Craft Organizer with Pony Craft Containers provide quick-view access, as do Flambeau Products' ArtBin's Clear View Storage Boxes and Leeco/Cropper Hopper's Embellishment Organizers. TidyCraft's Tidy Trays also provide easy corralling and pouring of tiny baubles.

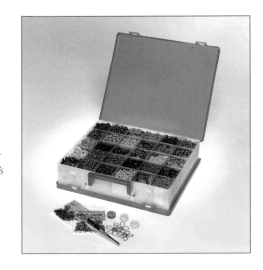

yarn together on the same cardstock "bobbin" or on separate bobbins in the same container.

- Some scrapbookers prefer to separate the individual color strands of fibers that come in multi-packs, while others prefer to keep them together as packaged. Use the method that best suits your scrapbooking style.

- Try not to bunch textiles which makes them wrinkle. Winding them around a bobbin or cardstock square is a better option.

- Floss boxes come with embroidery floss winding cards or bobbins. Wind one fiber type on each card. File these mini cards in the floss box by color. Each box can hold dozens of these small, fiber-wrapped cards. You can also place the bobbins in sticker sleeves in binders.

- Store textiles in compartmentalized boxes or cases, pocketed totes or in binders inside sticker protectors.

Eagle Affiliates' The Cross-Stitch Case and SCS/Hemline's Embroidery Thread Organizer help tame fibers when used with Uniek's plastic or SCS/Hemline's cardboard "bobbins." For quick winding of fibers onto bobbins, try Westex Corporations' Floss Winder.

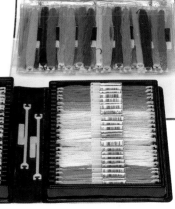

Keep embroidery floss sorted and under control with DMC's StitchBox™ Floss Holders, stored in the company's Organizing & Storage Binders and Cases (above). Plaid's Creative Gear™ Floss & Bobbin Holder tote provides on-the-go floss containment.

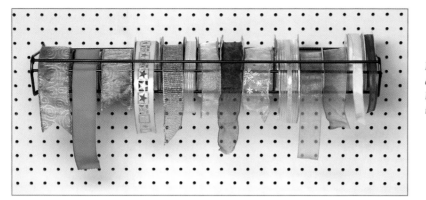

Novelcrafts' sticker dispenser for pegboard pulls double-duty keeping rolls of ribbon organized and ready for use. It's great for keeping large rolls of stickers organized and ready for use, too!

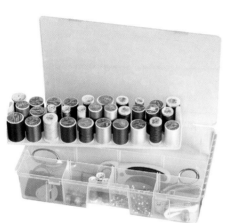

If you stitch on scrapbook pages, either by hand or by machine, you'll appreciate SCS/Hemline's Sewing Supplies Organizer (right), ArtBin's Sew-Lutions™ (above) and Bobbin Boxes. Tutto's Bobbin & Needlecraft Holder tote makes it easy to travel with threads.

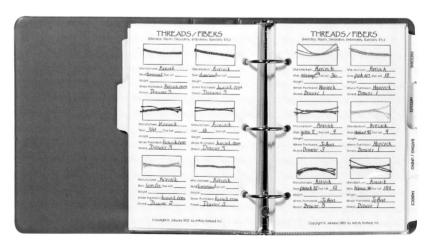

Use Artfully Scribed's Stitch-A-Log™ to help organize your fiber, floss and thread collections. The pre-printed three-ring binder even has a section for recording your favorite "master" stitches.

ORGANICS

Organic materials add a touch of nature to scrapbook albums. However, care and storage of organic materials—like cork sheets, feathers, pressed flowers, sand, shells, skeletonized leaves and tree bark—are an ongoing challenge. But these natural elements are definitely worth the extra effort. Here are some tips to help guide you.

- Keep all natural materials dry.

- Encase flowers and loose petals in vellum envelopes, plastic memorabilia envelopes and pockets or in separate areas where they will not harm photos if they crumble or shed seeds.

- Allow flowers to dry at least three months in open air before placing them in a storage container or scrapbook so that any tiny insect eggs can hatch and any microscopic insects will leave the organic matter.

- Shells, sand, twigs, bark and other organic items should be encapsulated in memorabilia pockets, plastic envelopes, or well-sealed shaker boxes.

- Shells should be allowed to dry naturally for two months in open air before you store them in containers or use them in a scrapbook. This allows the body of the animal to decompose inside the shell and not cause odors.

- Twigs and bark may cause staining of page elements due to wood tannins. If you use them in scrapbooking, allow them to dry for at least two months before storage or use. Keep them at least 4" away from photographs.

- Sort and group like items together.

- Whenever possible, keep organic materials flat and stable. Many are delicate and will break in too large storage containers that allow excessive movement.

- Store organic materials in zippered bags, flat boxes or cases or memorabilia keepers until you are ready to use them.

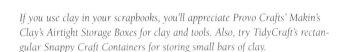

If you use clay in your scrapbooks, you'll appreciate Provo Crafts' Makin's Clay's Airtight Storage Boxes for clay and tools. Also, try TidyCraft's rectangular Snappy Craft Containers for storing small bars of clay.

For storing organic scrapbooking materials, stick with containers that provide little movement of materials as many organics are delicate. We like Akro-Mils' Craft Organizer Caddy, Flex Products' Flexanizers™ tubes and boxes, 3L's Memorabilia Pockets and C-Thru Ruler Company's Déjà Views® 3D Keepers.

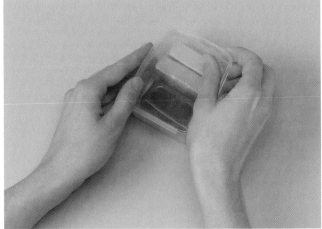

Keep your clays soft, supple and ready to use by "burping" containers to remove any excess air in them before closing tightly.

Inspirations

The inspirations and ideas that you rely on for scrapbook page design, page titles and journaling come in many forms and from many sources. Scrapbookers find inspiration from books, magazines, Internet Web sites, calendars, greeting cards, fabric or wallpaper swatches, napkin designs and the world around them. Some inspirations are printed from the computer, photocopied, photographed or simply torn from magazines. Other forms may include . Learn how to make a molehill out these "paper prompter" mountains. Knowing exactly where your page ideas are filed will save you half the time when you need to do the actual page layout. Being able to retrieve the idea when you need it is the secret to good organization.

Store punch art, theme, technique and general interest scrapbooking books in Highsmith's Colorful Magazine Files, which can be decorated as you wish to identify the different types of books you have.

IDEA BOOKS & MAGAZINES

Books and magazines can accumulate rapidly, especially if you are an avid subscriber. There are things you can do to stay on top of these types of inspiration.

- Avoid letting new idea books and magazines stack up in piles for "later." Later is an elusive beast often hard to find. Go through books and magazines within a week of receiving them and affix sticky notes only to the pages you really want to re-create.

- To easily identify a page theme, try color-coding page ideas with different colored sticky notes. For example, use pink or blue to tag baby pages, yellow to tag travel pages, green to tag Christmas, orange to tag autumn pages, etc. Use the same color coding system to tag other sources of inspiration, such as those listed on the following pages.

- Some magazine publishers' Web sites have indexes for the past year's article topics. Print these out and store them with that year's magazines for quick reference.

- Some scrapbookers opt to avoid the storage of periodicals altogether by simply tearing out the ideas or techniques they like. Ideas are then pasted on a sheet of typing paper and sorted, organized, labeled and inserted into a binder. They then pitch the magazine.

- If color-coding pages with sticky notes or tearing magazine pages out is not for you, try scanning page ideas that you want to re-create. Print them out as 4 x 5" images in black-and-white. File in an index-card file or keep them in a binder sorted, organized and labeled by theme or season . Label with a reference to the issue date, number and page so you can find the original if needed.

- Do not keep a "miscellaneous" file section. It will get too big and too broad to be useful.

- Regardless of the organizational system you choose for books and magazines, file the ideas right away. Keep only the layout concepts you know you will use in due time.

Avoid letting new idea books and magazines stack up in piles for "later." Some magazine publishers manufacture specialty binders in which to store their scrapbook magazines.

- Sort and organize magazines by month, year or publisher. Some scrapbookers store their magazines in groups by month regardless of publisher, which enables them to find seasonal ideas quickly.

- Try organizing a year's worth of magazines in chronological order. Then photocopy each index page and file all twelve of these in the front of the yearly section.

- Create a database in a word-processing program that indicates your favorite page layouts and which pages they are on in certain books or magazines.

- Sort your magazines yearly. You will be surprised how your tastes change over time. Do not keep every magazine you buy. If you have outgrown everything in a magazine, gift it to a new scrapbooker, sell it on an Internet auction or at a garage sale.

- Store magazines in publisher-manufactured three-ring binders in bookcases or on open shelving.

- Sort and organize idea books by topic. Group theme books (wedding, baby, toddler, school, travel, heritage, etc.), how-to technique books (paper crafts, photo cropping, punch art, rubber stamping, etc.) and general interest (basic scrapbooking topics, like this book) together for storing.

- Books should be stored on end with spines facing you.

- Take your favorite "used often" idea books to an office-supply store and have them spliced and spiral bound. This allows them to lie flat without harming the spine.

POEMS, QUOTES & SAYINGS

Poems, quotes or sayings may link your mind to a set of photos you already have or photos you would like to take. These inspirational words easily become page titles and journaling blocks. If you enjoy researching and saving these words of wisdom, put a good organizational system in place so you can find them when you need them.

- Use a word-processing program to keep a database file in your computer and add quotes you like to it. Sort the lists by season and theme.

- Keep a section in a scrapbook inventory binder (see page 48) for your poems, page title ideas, quotes and sayings, or keep them in a separate binder.

- Print poems, quotes and sayings that you love immediately onto vellum as a 4 x 5" size. File these "ready to use" vellum words by theme with your other pre-made page additions. Use as you would other pre-made sentiments, sticker poems and titles for quick pages.

- Print poems out as simple text documents and file in hanging files by topic. You can later retype them in fonts you prefer.

- Use a diskette or reusable CD to store poetry you find online. Keep it near the computer and update it as needed. You can also create a CD for each season. Add all the Christmas, valentine and snow poems to the "winter poetry" CD. Retrieve them from the CD as needed.

- Keep a "poems, quotes and sayings" notebook in your own handwriting, divided by season or theme.

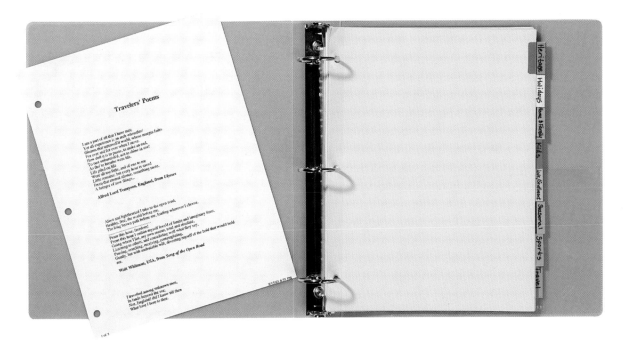

Store sorted poems, quotes and sayings by theme in Kokuyo's Color 'N' Color Collection three-ring binders. Use notebook dividers to separate theme categories.

PAGE SKETCHES

If you're one of those talented scrapbookers with the artistic ability to sketch out page design layouts, the following ideas may help keep them organized.

- Sketch your own layout ideas on blank paper or index cards.

- File idea index cards according to either theme, supplies used, or number of photos used. Use the same type of labeling system if storing ideas in a binder.

- Tack sketches up on large bulletin boards or room divider screens for quick reference if you intend to create the page in the very near future.

Page sketches on index cards store nicely in General Box Company's Decorate Me™ boxes, decorated how and wherever your whimsy takes you.

PERSONAL MEMORIES

Personal memories and notes about events from your life and the lives of loved ones are numerous. Use these ideas to help preserve and document these memories, with the ultimate goal of getting these memories into a scrapbook album to share with others.

- Keep a daily journal or a journal that you write in after each photographic event. Note the date, place, and people as well as any emotions, happy or sad happenings, or memories from the event. Jot down your thoughts. You don't have to use all of this information in a family scrapbook but it will be a good device to jog your memory when you do make the scrapbook page.

- Keep a "snapshot log" with your camera. Each time you return the camera to its storage spot, jot down notes from the snapshot session just completed.

- Tape recordings, recorder buttons and videotapes are great devices for recording the elder generation. Interview them at length and transcribe the notes for later. See page 40 for care, organization and storage of audio- and videotapes.

- Keep computer text files in a word-processing program. Memories can either be verbose or simple; from rough notes to elegant essays. Keep track of the feelings behind the events. You can even import poems, quotes or images into the file for later use.

- Jot short blurbs down on sticky notes and attach them to the backs of photos as soon as they are printed.

- Never throw away your annual calendars or day planners. They hold a wellspring of information about the events of a year. Get in the habit of recording as much information about daily life as possible on a calendar and store the calendar with that year's photographs to help jog memories about dates, times and events.

OTHER SOURCES OF INSPIRATION

Wherever you find words, shapes, color and texture, you will find page design inspiration! You can find "photos to take" ideas, journaling or graphic concepts in advertisements, billboards, cartoons, catalogs, children's story books, clip art, clothing, coloring books, gift wrap, greeting cards, t-shirts, wall paper and borders. Keep track of these noteworthy inspirations for quick reference.

- Trim tear sheets with scissors.

- Sort and group these inspirations by themes or topics.

- Paste ideas onto index cards and store in an index-card file or on notebook paper stored in a binder.

- Label card file or notebook dividers as you label any other source of information, color-coding as needed to keep your organized inspiration system easily identified and united.

To help with journaling on scrapbook pages, get in the habit of keeping a daily journal, saving annual calendars and attaching sticky notes right away to the backs of photos when you get the prints from your photo lab.

If you collect design and quote inspirations from sources like greeting cards, catalogs, etc., you'll find it helpful to trim them down and paste on index cards by theme. Then use file card dividers to keep them sorted by theme. As you tear out new inspirations, immediately paste them on the cards to avoid clutter.

Paper

Paper is one of the most important staples in a scrapbooker's arsenal of tools and supplies. It comes in hundreds of colors, patterns, textures and weights and is sold by single sheet or in packets, pads or booklets. Paper plays a vital role in scrapbook page design and it is one of the most enjoyable items to shop for at the store. You may have a lot of paper or a just a little. Either way, you need to know how to take care of it so that it gets from the store to the completed scrapbook page in good condition.

- Keep your paper in a clean, dry place away from direct sunlight.

- Ideal temperatures for paper storage are between 65 to 80 degrees Fahrenheit, with low to moderate humidity.

- To be photo-safe, paper should be pH neutral (acid-free) and lignin-free.

- Many varieties are buffered, which is preferable for scrapbooking projects.

- Keep insects away from your papers.

- Pets and small children can cause a lot of turmoil with a paper stack. Keep your paper out of reach of children and family pets.

- Sort and group solid-colored paper and cardstock using the "ROYGBIV" rainbow order. This is Red, Orange, Yellow, Green, Blue, Indigo and Violet. Add black, gray, white, cream, brown and tans to the front or the back end of the filing spectrum.

- Sort and group patterned papers by design theme (see list on page 73) for easier access.

- Not all vellum, mulberry, metallic or handmade papers are archivally safe and, as such, should not be allowed to directly touch photos and memorabilia on a scrapbook page or be stored with acid-free, archival-safe papers.

For small or portable paper collections, try Kokuyo's Paper Kaddy (available in two sizes), Leeco/Cropper Hopper's Paper Organizer, Mochalatte's Scrapping & Accessories Organizer, Caren's Crafts' Scrap-N-File Photomate™ and Scrap-N-File™ Original, Generations' 12 x 12" Scrapfolio™ or Plaid® Creative Gear's Expandable File.

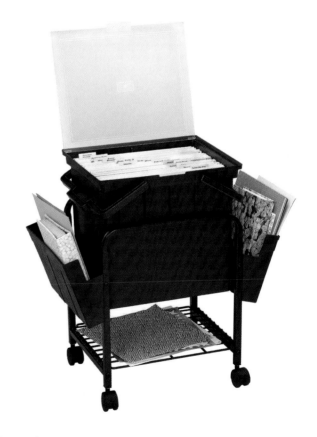

Plastic paper totes come in mainly in two styles: those with and those without dividers, as in the case of Leeco/Cropper Hopper's 12 x 12" Paper Organizers.

If you prefer vertical paper storage, Leeco/Cropper Hopper's 12 x 12" Heavy Duty Workstation allows for simple sort-and-drop filing. The unit holds over 4,000 sheets of paper.

- If you have a significant collection of vellum, mulberry, metallic or handmade papers, sort by color and/or theme. Otherwise, a simple folder or drawer for each paper type may suffice.

- For booklets of paper, you have a number of organization options. You can keep the paper bound in the booklet until ready to use and just organize the booklets on a shelf or in a 12 x 12" binder by theme. Or tear the patterned sheets from the booklet and incorporate into the rest of your sorted patterned or specialty papers.

- When you identify papers you no longer wish to use for scrapbooking, they can be used for wrapping small gifts, making greeting cards or other craft projects.

- Create a "give-away" folder filled with papers you no longer care for anymore. When the folder is full, give it to a charity or a scrapbooking friend.

- Store your paper in a manner that makes it easy for you to find it again. If you like to work by manufacturer, sort that way. If you work by theme, sort your patterned papers that way.

- Paper can be stored in a wide variety of ways. Store paper horizontally whenever possible. For horizontal storage, store paper flat in corrugated cardboard, wire, wood or acrylic paper racks, trays or shallow drawer units.

- For vertical storage, store paper upright in magazine file boxes, accordion files, hanging files in cropping bins or file drawers, or in paper cases and totes. If storing paper vertically, keep it snugly filed so it does not curl or "hunch" over.

- When storing paper on wire racks, make inexpensive dust covers from bed sheeting. Fasten fabric to wire racks with heavy-duty glue dots.

- Secure tall racks to the wall, if possible, to prevent toppling.

- Take a sample sheet of scrapbooking paper along with you when you shop for storage containers. You can test the fit before you buy.

- Keep a 12 x 12" paper keeper in your car for unexpected shopping trips to keep the paper in tip-top shape until you get it home.

There are many options, styles and sizes available for wire paper storage solutions, including Novelcrafts' Scrapbook Displays (black) and Caren's Crafts' Stack-N-File™ Hanging File System. Take precautions to ensure that small children cannot climb on or topple over tall paper racks and towers.

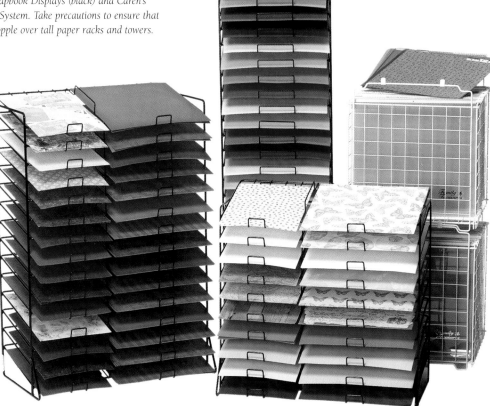

Patterned paper categories

You'll find that you can sort, group and/or organize most all of your patterned paper into the following theme categories. As a general rule, the more paper you have, the more precise you'll need your categories. The less paper you have, the more broad your categories can be. Perhaps you'll find themes or categories that we haven't even thought of!

Amusement Park/Carnival	Patriotic
Animals or pets	Picnic/BBQ
Autumn	Plaids
Baby	Pool
Beach	Religious
Birthday	School
Camping/fishing	Scouting
Celebrations	Seasonal
Chanukah	Snow
Characters	Sports
Christmas	Spring
Disney	Stripes
Dots	Summer
Easter	Swirls
Feminine	Teen
Floral	Texture
Gardening	Thanksgiving
Halloween	Travel
Heritage/Victorian	Wedding
Holidays	Winter
Masculine	Zoo
Nature and outdoors	

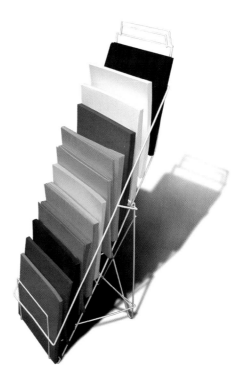

DMD's 12 x 12" Paper Pack Rack provides upright paper storage. It is also available in an 8½ x 11" model.

Specialty papers

You'll find that most of your specialty papers will fall into one of the following categories:

Handmade	Suede
Metallic	Vellum
Mulberry	Woodgrain

For those who prefer acid-free cardboard paper storage, a couple of options include Highsmith's 12 x 12" Supply Chest (left) and 8½ x 11" Paper Keeper (center). For smaller or specialty paper collections, try Generations' Memory Express™. For the fun of it, all can be decorated and embellished to suit your personal style.

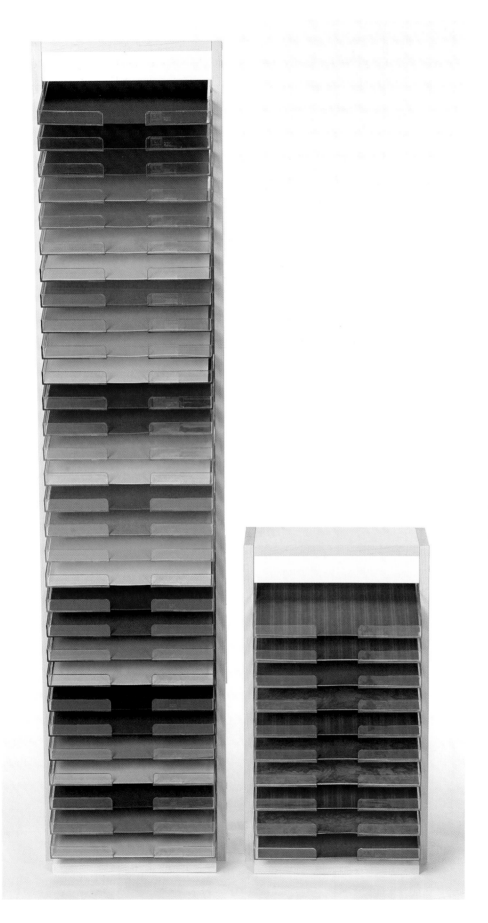

Another paper storage option is Display Dynamics' flexible, stackable clear plastic paper trays and wood laminate towers. The Paper Station has enough space to hold 30 trays, while the Paper Station Mini can accommodate 10 trays. Both models are available in 12 x 12" and 8½ x 11" sizes. The stations can stand on floors, desktops or anywhere you keep paper. Display Dynamics' also has free-standing, stackable trays in both popular paper sizes. With tall paper racks and towers, take precautions to ensure that small children cannot climb on them or topple them over.

PAPER SCRAPS

Scrapbooking generates a lot of bits and pieces of paper scraps. Those little scraps come in awfully handy for creating punch art, photo corners, mats, journaling blocks and other page accents. Keeping paper scraps organized will ensure that they get used thus getting the most bang for your scrapbook buck.

- Dump out your entire lot of scrap papers. Use a pair of scissors to trim off any frayed, bent or awkward edges to make containment easier.

- As if you're dealing a deck of cards, sort scraps into piles by color family. It isn't necessary to separate out solid and patterned papers. Simply "deal" each scrap into the following piles: white/white patterns, black and black/gray patterns, brown/brown patterns, cream/cream patterns, red/red patterns, orange/orange patterns, yellow/yellow patterns, green/green patterns, blue/blue patterns and violet/violet patterns.

- Sort specialty papers by group (see type categories on page 73) or intermix types and sort by color. Remember not to store archival papers with specialty papers.

- Once all scraps are sorted determine the most suitable-sized storage container for your scraps.

- Paper scrap storage options include drawer units, vertical hanging file folders and accordion files. Be sure to label each category of paper color for at-a-glance locating.

- If desired, cut scraps into 3 x 3" or 4 x 4" journaling squares, $4\frac{1}{2}$ x $6\frac{1}{2}$" photo mats and 2" squares. Punch jumbo and mega squares and circles for future use in page titles or accents. File these precut paper blocks in rainbow-color order with your pre-made page accents (see following page).

- Throw away paper scraps that are no larger than 2 x 2".

You'd be amazed at how much additional use you can get out of paper scraps when they are organized. Store in accordion-style keepers such as Caren's Crafts' Scrap-N-Sticker Border File™ (which also works great for stickers!).

PRE-MADE PAGE ADDITIONS

Next to paper and embellishments, pre-made page additions are likely to be your largest collection of mass chaos among your scrapbooking supplies. There's a reason why these collections grow so fast; they look smashing on scrapbook pages and help make scrapbook page design quick and easy. That is, of course, if you can find your page additions.

A pre-made page addition comes in many forms and can include anything that you add to a page as a decorative accent, design element, title or journaling block, border, frame or corner design. See the list on the next for paper items that could be considered a page addition.

For scrapbooking efficiency, organize all of your page additions by theme—not by type of supply or by product manufacturer. For example, when you create a winter page layout, find all of your "winter" accents quickly in the "winter" section of your page additions or use the patterned paper categories on page 73. These tips will help:

- Store page additions flat, either horizontally or vertically. Possible storage containers include accordion-type files, large envelopes, file folders, plastic drawer units, or binders outfitted with page protectors.

- Glue die cuts or other page additions onto blank sheets of paper by theme with removable/repositionable adhesive. Store these sheets by theme category in page protectors within binders.

- Use a 12 x 12" or 8½ x 11" three-ring binder for page addition storage. Binders with page protectors and photo sleeves will fit all sizes of page additions or die cuts. Your binder can be stored in your file drawer, large tote or bin, or on the desk.

- Store paper die-cut shapes in boxes, accordion files, hanging files, tilt bins, binders, plastic zippered sandwich bags held on a ring, or inexpensive 4 x 6" photo albums—sorted and organized by theme.

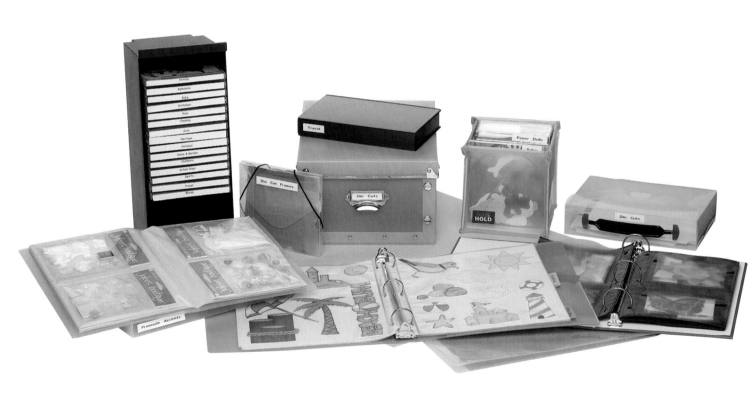

There are many ways to store organized pre-made page additions and die cuts. Try Kokuyo's photo albums with cases, Leeco's Media File Bin outfitted with jewel cases, Traffic Works' corded storage boxes, VHS "clamshell" cases, Kokuyo's large E-Z Snap boxes, Inventor's Studio's Fold 'N Hold mesh caddy outfitted with CD jewel cases, Traffic Works' handled storage boxes, Light Impressions' Slimline CD Album with protective sleeves or Kokuyo's Color 'N' Color Collection binder with page protectors.

WHAT'S A PRE-MADE PAGE ADDITION?

- 3-D stickers
- Blank journaling boxes
- Border accents
- Decorative elements
- Die cuts
- Frames
- Handmade page accents
- Laser-cut frames
- Page "toppers" and titles

- Paper dolls
- Paper piecings
- Paper-folding patterns
- Paper-piecing patterns
- Preprinted poems
- Punch art or punched pieces
- Stickers
- Tags

PAGE ADDITION THEMES

Finding an element quickly is the object of page-addition organization and sorting by themes is one of the most efficient methods. Divide your page additions into at least four seasonal categories. The more page additions you have, the more theme categories you will need. Keep your theme categories in alphabetical order. If you have more than 10 pages of one theme, break it into subcategories. For example, Autumn can become Halloween, Thanksgiving, Autumn Activities, etc. Or Winter can be broken down into Christmas, New Year's, Wintry Activities, and so on. Pick and choose from these suggested themes, depending on what best describes your page-addition collection, or use the themes on page 73 for sorting.

- Animals/Pets/Zoo
- Baby/Small children
- Bible/Religion
- Birthday/Celebration/Party
- Camping/Hiking
- Christmas
- Computers/Technology
- Disney
- Eras—1970s, 1980s, 1990s, etc.
- Fall/Leaves/Halloween
- Floral/Garden
- Food/Dishes/Teapots
- Hearts
- Heritage/Victorian

- Hobbies/Scrapbooking/ Quilting/Tools
- Holidays (Choose the holidays that suit your family)
- Music/Stage/Dance
- Paper dolls (Blank and not dressed—no theme yet)
- School/Artist/Graduation
- Scouting
- Sports
- Summer/Sun/Sandals
- Trees/Large Shrubs
- Travel/Vehicles
- Water/Beach/Pool
- Wedding
- Winter/Snow

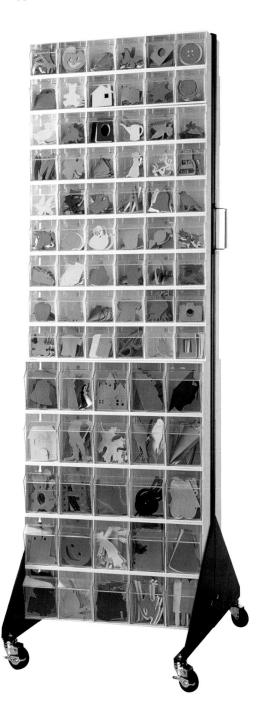

For large die-cut and page-addition collections, Quantum Storage Systems' special Die Cut Centers come in two varieties: wall-mounted or mobile, like the one shown at left.

Stickers can be an immense part of your scrapbooking supply collection. They vary in theme, size and style and can pose an organizational challenge. There are, however, some great ways to organize and store the stickers you have without crushing or damaging them. Once you get your stickers and page additions organized, you'll know just where to find them for photo mats, borders, page accents, journaling blocks, corners, on pop ups, and inside large die-cut cardstock letters. Follow these convenient tips for taming your sticker collection:

- Sort your stickers into themes.

- Use the right-sized storage device. Stuffing a 12" inch sticker into an 11" space will end in crushing and crumpling your supplies.

- Put away stickers promptly after purchase or scrapbooking to prevent damage or loss.

- Give each theme and size of sticker its own home within your filing system.

- Store your letter and number stickers separately from your theme and picture-style stickers.

- Sliding your stickers into page protectors or slip-in sleeves of some kind will protect them better than having them loose in a file system where edges will catch and sticker strips will come loose and adhere to their neighbors.

- Sticker storage containers include sticker binders produced by sticker manufacturers; storage cases with index cards as dividers; page protectors in three-ring binders; slip-in, sleeve-style photo album refill pages for 4 x 6" and 5 x 7" photos (for smaller stickers); accordion-style file organizers or hanging files in cabinets.

Sticker storage options include Highsmith's Sticker Keeper, ready for you to decorate; Caren's Crafts' accordion-style Scrap-N-Sticker Border File™; Leeco/Cropper Hopper's Sticker Case and Generations' Craft Keeper pockets, to name a few. For "drop system" storage, try Making Memories' hanging file folders.

Uses for extra stickers

When sorting stickers, you may come across a few you no longer like for scrapbooking. Use them in a variety of ways around the home.

- Spruce up plain gift bags and plain butcher paper by adding stickers. Vary the theme for each gift bag or sheet of gift wrap.

- Give them to your youngster. He or she will love playing with them.

- Donate them as a scrapbooking door prize at the next crop you attend.

- Make greeting cards. It only takes a few stickers and a few pieces of cardstock to make an elegant card.

- Place the stickers on reward charts or chore charts for your children or grandchildren.

- Add them to the school carnival prize bucket.

- Place them on your outgoing bills and letters to brighten a mail handler's day.

- Swap, donate or sell them (see page 34).

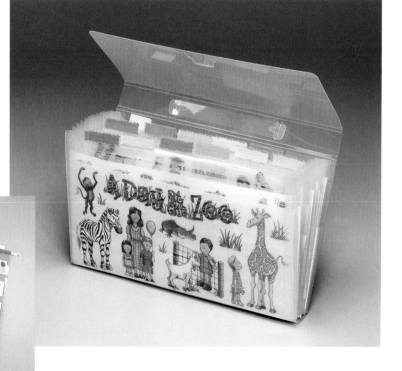

Crop In Style's zippered Paper/Sticker Binder (PSB), outfitted with the company's acid- and PVC-free inserts, is sure to fit your sticker storing needs.

Leeco/Cropper Hopper manufactures a number of sticker storage options, including a 7 x 12" Expandable Organizer and an Oversized Organizer. The company's 12 x 12" Hanging Sticker Sheet Variety Packs drop right into their 12 x 12" Heavy Duty Workstation for vertical sticker storage.

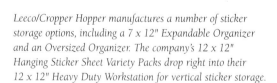

ALTERNATIVE WORKSPACE & STORAGE OPTIONS

You now have fairly good exposure to the wide variety of wonderful storage products and units designed specifically for scrapbookers. While a visit to the local scrapbook or container store will reveal a plethora of storage and containment ideas, there are plenty of less-expensive substitutes as well if you are on a fairly tight budget.

Selecting the right storage unit can be an overwhelming task at first, but if you have experience organizing a household or an office, many of the same principles apply. In fact, many of the same storage materials that you use to organize household and office supplies come in handy in a scrapbook workspace.

In this chapter you will learn about a variety of places where you can find frugal yet effective storage solutions. You will discover how to comb a flea market for inexpensive storage supplies. You will also find suggestions for incorporating antiques into your workspace and tips for converting ordinary household items into sensational storage containers.

In no time at all, you will have a place for everything so that you can finally put everything in its proper place!

At the flea market, bring lots of small bills and be prepared to wade through aisles and aisles of boxes, bins and booths in search of storage containers. Don't get sidetracked by all of the other stuff. Stay on goal.

Frugal Flea-Market Finds

Flea markets can be a storage and container "treasure trove." Flea markets can also be a financial downfall if you are a spontaneous shopper who loves to buy anything fun that catches your eye. The key to successful flea-market shopping is to stay focused on finding products you truly need.

To prove that an effective workspace can be pulled together quickly and economically, three *Memory Makers* staffers—Senior Book Editor MaryJo Regier, Executive Magazine Editor Debbie Mock and Staff Photographer Ken Trujillo—visited a local flea market to test their shopping prowess. Their mission? To stock a complete workspace for $100 or less.

PREPARATION

To get the very best deals possible, staffers made the following preparations before hitting the flea market. These ideas will help you be more successful at the flea market as well.

- First they assessed their scrapbooking tools and supplies and storage containers and needs (see shopping list on following page).

- Then they set a budget and agreed to bargain as much as possible in an effort to spend $100 or less.

- The workspace area's height, width and depth were measured and recorded. The measurements and a tape measure were taken to the flea market to avoid the frustration of purchasing an item that would be too big for the space.

- The team decided to take MaryJo's van for hauling purchases back to the office.

STAYING FOCUSED

Our staff shoppers put on their proverbial "horse blinders" before walking down the flea market aisles. The team had to resist the temptation to purchase paintbrushes, make-up sponges, etc.—many of which cost less than a dollar—and focus on the goal at hand: to find items in which they could store their scrapbooking supplies. "If you keep repeating 'store and contain' over and over to yourself, it will help you stick to your mission of finding organizational containers," says MaryJo.

Don't be too shy to get right in there and dig down into a seller's wares. Sometimes the best storage treasures are hidden deep!

HAVING PATIENCE

Shopping a flea market is not the fastest process, but it can reap huge rewards. Staffers wore their best walking shoes so that they were prepared to walk the entire market. Oftentimes they found an item that seemed almost right but not perfect. Rather than purchasing it on the spot, they moved on, noting where in the market the item was located, in case they decided to return later on.

BEING PERSISTENT

Things at the flea market were not always organized. Staffers made sure to dig into bins and to scan each booth to make sure they didn't overlook any shelves or tables. Sometimes the biggest treasures were hidden deep!

FINDING PERSPECTIVE

Our staffers found that not everything at the flea market was a bargain. Some items could be found at a lower price at discount or office supply stores. In other cases, the quality of the products at the flea market was compromised and purchasing these items new at a store, even if they cost a little more money, made sense. As Debbie explains, "If you can pick up a sturdy new table at a home store for $50, it will probably be a better investment than a wobbly $15 table from the flea market."

Debbie and MaryJo examine countless containers, weighing how functional and useful they would or wouldn't be in a scrapbook workspace. If an item is not going to be useful and solve an immediate storage problem, don't buy it. You'll just add to your existing clutter.

Flea market shopping list

Here's the preliminary shopping list the team took to the flea market:

- Card table to be used as a work surface
- A lamp or light
- Makeup case for embellishments and tools on-the-go
- Cigar boxes for pens
- Silverware cases, trays or caddies for embellishments and tools on-the-go
- VHS "clamshell" cases for die cuts or pens
- CD-ROM jewel cases for die cuts, stickers or "punchies"
- Plastic or clear containers with lids—preferably stackable; some compartmentalized—for punches, decorative scissors, colorants, tools, pens, stamps or embellishments
- Stackable spice jars for embellishments

- Small, compartmentalized toolbox for tools or cleaners
- Baskets for idea books and magazines
- Wooden compartmentalized cabinets or shelves for stamp storage
- Kitchen utility carousels or spoon holders for most commonly used work surface tools
- Office storage pieces or bins to place atop, beneath or beside work surface
- Small file cabinet
- Small bookshelf
- Small sheet of pegboard with hooks
- Bulletin board
- Any container or caddy with handles for cropping on-the-go

ASSESSING POTENTIAL

Before purchasing any item, staffers asked themselves several questions. Is the item in good condition (or can it at least be easily fixed)? Is it large enough for my needs or will I outgrow it quickly? Will it work well with other containers I already have? Will it have an immediate impact on my mission of getting organized? If they answered "no" to any of these questions, they moved on to the next booth.

HAGGLING

Staffers kept a "cool head and a poker face," says Debbie. They carried cash in small bills so that they could make quick and easy purchases. They kept in mind a price they were willing to pay for an item and were not afraid to haggle or to walk away if negotiations were not successful.

THE FINAL INVOICE

At the end of the day, the team triumphantly returned to the office with everything they needed to create a highly functional scrapbook workspace. Here's a list of MaryJo, Debbie and Ken's expenses for the day, including flea-market admission, shopping cart rental and lunch. The final cost of their shopping spree? Just $68.50—well under their starting budget of $100.

Our flea market finds	
Budget	$ 100.00
flea market admission	3.00
Shopping cart rental	2.00
Lunch	14.75
Folding table	5.00
Sm. fabric-covered caddy	1.00
Sign (impulse buy)	.75
Nuts and bolts drawer unit	2.00
Crisscross accordion hanger	1.00
4 mini Rubbermaid containers	1.50
Polka-dot bag on wheels	4.00
Over-the-door hanger	1.00
Yellow multipurpose caddy	1.00
Wood/acrylic wall-display shelves	1.00
Old wooden crate	7.00
Brown office chair	8.00
Lazy Susan	1.00
Paper storage compartment	1.00
Decorative jars	1.00
Two 3-ring notebooks	1.00
Silverware tray	.50
Wooden cigar box	1.00
Large tackle box	5.00
CD tote	4.00
Portable paper file	1.00
Total spent	$ 68.50

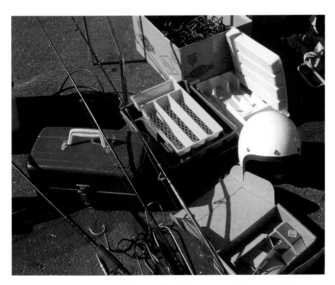

Negotiate on prices and walk away if a seller is not ready to come down. Perhaps he'll change his mind later. And when a storage product is just perfect, you'll know it—such as these old spice racks, a "lazy susan" turntable and a straight-sided silverware tray.

Before:

What a mess! When tired staffers arrived back at the office, they triumphantly piled up their purchases, but the workspace was far from ready to crop in. With a little elbow grease, cleaning and decorating...

After:

...the frugal flea market finds became a functional workspace. Everything has been labeled and organized supplies have been stocked in the containers. One could just sit down and make a scrapbook page!

Antiques in the Workspace

While the primary purpose of a scrapbook workspace is functionality, there is no reason why it cannot be beautiful as well. Many scrapbookers depend on the clean lines of contemporary, modular furniture for scrapbooking, but other scrapbookers prefer a more traditional look to blend in with their home decor.

Sound expensive? Antiques don't have to be. Survey your home for older furniture, or shop local flea markets and secondhand thrift stores. You might even inherit a piece or two from other family members.

Here's how some of our readers have incorporated used-but-not-abused and hand-me-down furniture into their scrapbook workspaces.

Betsy Bell Sammarco (New Canaan, Connecticut) uses a piece of historic American furniture—the Hoosier cabinet—as a workspace and to organize her scrapbooking supplies. Hoosier cabinets were commonly found in early 20th-century kitchens. They were multifunctional—serving as pie safes, kitchen tables, cutting boards and dough boards. Many had drawers, hooks, spice racks, sugar jars and flour sifters as well in order to to make a housewife's job easier in the kitchen.

The top doors of Betsy's cabinet open to a shelved area which holds her magazines and idea books. To the left of these doors is a metal flour sifter, which she uses as a trash can. The outside of the sifter holds her "to do" lists and other notes with magnets. Hidden behind a center panel is a little shelf and a lot of room for storing punches, pens and scissors. The porcelain tabletop pulls out to become a large work surface. Under the tabletop to the left is a large bottom cabinet which holds her albums, paper, cutting mat and other large supplies. She hangs supplies from the metal bracket hanging from the inside door. To the right of this cabinet are three drawers. The top one is sectioned and holds her rulers, pencils and other supplies. The middle drawer holds stickers and the bottom drawer is large and perfect for larger size supplies. Betsy says that one of the best things about the cabinet is that it can be closed up when she is done working to conceal its contents and return to its glory being a beautiful antique in her home.

In Tricia Renner's (Leawood, Kansas) dining room at right is an optician's cabinet dating back to the early 1900s. The cabinet contains eighteen small, shallow drawers and ten large, shallow drawers—all of which are numbered. It was originally used to house a wide variety of eyeglass lenses, but nowadays it stores Tricia's paper, stickers and supplies. Tricia says that the cabinet is a super place for organization of supplies and doubles as a great piece of furniture.

Connie Mieden Cox's (Westminster, Colorado) workspace is a wonderful combination of contemporary and used furniture. Mixed in with the plastic modular storage units are two antique library card-catalog cabinets and an art-deco-style kitchen cupboard that she purchased at an antique store. She created a scrapbook-themed bulletin board by refinishing an ornate antique picture frame that she found at a flea market. An old air-drying clothes rack has been given new life as a hanger for large sheets of paper. And her favorite antique spice racks now store beads, baubles and other tiny embellishments.

Found Around the House

If you're in a budget quandary, you often need not look further than your own home to find a container in which to stash supplies. A quick survey of your kitchen, bathroom, home office and other rooms will provide organizational storage opportunities. Want to make your workspace personalized as well as functional? Use your well-honed scrapbooking skills to decorate "found" storage containers with stickers or patterned papers. Here's just a few ideas:

ADHESIVES

- Baskets

CROPPING-ON-THE-GO

- Cosmetic bags
- Large makeup cases
- Tackle and tool boxes

DECORATIVE SCISSORS

- Belt and tie racks

EMBELLISHMENTS

- Baby food jars
- Clear, empty film canisters
- Small, compartmentalized tackle boxes
- Small drawer units
- Seven-day pill organizers
- Snack-size plastic baggies with zippered closings
- Spice rack with jars

IDEA BOOKS & MAGAZINES

- Crates

MISCELLANEOUS TOOLS

- Magnetic kitchen utensil rack
- Plastic bins
- Plastic food storage containers
- Silverware caddy

PAPER AND PRE-MADE PAGE ACCENTS

- CD-ROM "clamshells"

- Empty, clean pizza box

- Kids' baseball card holders

- Letter-size accordion files

- Plastic milk-crate box filled with letter-size folders

- Under-the-bed storage box

PENS, PENCILS & MARKERS

- Canning jars

- Coffee mugs

- Flowerpot with drainage hole plugged

- Old make-up bags

- Pencil cases

- Revolving office supply caddy

- Straight-sided silverware-drawer organizers

- Vases

- VHS tape "clamshell" cases

PUNCHES & STAMPS

- Clear and deep acrylic picture frames with the backing removed

- Compartmentalized tackle or tool boxes

- Emptied-out silverware case

- Large plastic storage containers with lids

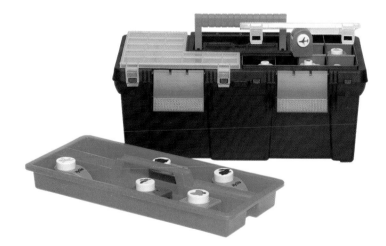

MAINTAINING WORKSPACE EFFICIENCY

Congratulations! What an accomplishment! Hopefully by now you have carefully inventoried your supplies, purchased economical storage units and stashed away your materials in an orderly fashion. And now you are eager to start using your space to create more scrapbook pages—the ultimate reward! But what happens once you begin to actually crop in your newly designed workspace? Or when you return from a shopping trip with a bag of new supplies? How about when you return home from cropping-on-the-go? These three activities—page creation, shopping and cropping-on-the-go are culprits when it comes to turning an orderly workspace back into disarray. But if you make a concerted effort to maintain your workspace after each page creation or shopping or cropping trip, you'll be blessed with a fresh start each time you sit down to scrapbook.

In this last chapter you will find guidelines for developing helpful organizational habits to help you maintain your scrapbook workspace, as well as tips for reviewing, rotating and replenishing supplies. You will discover how to get organized for efficient cropping-on-the-go, including how to make "page kits" for streamlined scrapbooking. You'll see numerous totes and carry-alls designed just for scrapbookers to help make your scrapbook trips comfortable and carefree. And as a grand finale, gain insight from two scrapbookers who traded scrapbook workspaces for a day and learned to view their own workspaces through fresh eyes.

Like a fine-tuned automobile, an effective scrapbook workspace requires ongoing maintenance. A little organization and few good habits will help you to go the distance!

Maintaining Your Workspace

Whether you scrapbook on a folding table, a kitchen counter or customized scrapbook station, maintaining your workspace is the best way to ensure unhampered creativity. These tips should help.

Tips for Staying Organized

CLEAR YOUR DESK

Before you start any scrapbooking session, make sure that your work surface is clutter-free.

TAKE OUT ONLY WHAT YOU NEED

Leave all unneeded tools and supplies tucked away so you have room to spread out. If you are working on a birthday page, place only your balloon print paper and cake die cuts in front of you. If you are working on punch art, take out your punches and cardstock.

CLEAN AS YOU GO

Keep a trash can next to your desk or tape a paper bag to the side of your table. As paper scraps pile up, be sure to deposit them. Upon finishing with each tool, put it back in its place. As you complete individual pages, place them in page protectors and file them away.

WRAP UP WITH A CLEAN SWEEP

When done scrapbooking, clear off paper scraps, wipe down your work surface, vacuum and take out the garbage.

SUPPLY REVIEW & ROTATION

As your scrapbooking style evolves, so too will your supply needs. Tools that were once essential may become obsolete. And items you once thought you'd never use may become staples. Periodically review and rotate your supplies to ensure maximum potential.

BE FLEXIBLE

It takes time to determine your scrapbooking requirements and trial and error to identify which supplies you really need. Don't hesitate to make changes when necessary.

FOR EVERYTHING, THERE IS A SEASON

Think of your supplies as your scrapbooking wardrobe. Change them with the seasons. Place out-of-season items in long-term storage until next year.

After you are done scrapbooking, clear off any random items, refile useable paper scraps, wipe down your work surface, vacuum up paper scraps from the floor and take out the garbage. Wrap up with a clean sweep!

SWAP WITH YOURSELF

If you have participated in a swap, you know the excitement of receiving a package filled with brand-new goodies. Experience that same excitement on your own. Instead of keeping all your embellishments close at hand, box some of them up and place them in a closet. Every few months, "swap" with yourself by taking some new items out of the box and putting others away.

WHEN IN DOUBT, THROW IT OUT

Don't hold onto supplies that you won't use. If something has been in storage for more than a year and you haven't wanted or needed it, then sell it, trade it or give it away.

Replenishing Supplies & Smart Shopping

One of the most enjoyable activities in scrapbooking is shopping, whether replenishing those supplies that have been used up, or purchasing just-on-the-market products. But in order not to clutter your workspace with unnecessary impulse purchases, it is important to balance what you want with what you truly need. These smart shopping tips will help:

BUDGET YOURSELF

Determine a budget and stick to it. This will help cut down on impulse purchases.

MAKE A LIST; CHECK IT TWICE

Before shopping, create a list of essential items you must replenish. Purchase these items first. Buy yourself a treat with money left over.

COMPARE PRICES

Shop around. Search catalogs, the Internet, and watch for sales for the best bargains.

WHAT'S IT WORTH TO YOU?

Before purchasing a new item, consider its price and usefulness. That paper punch may only cost $10, but if you use it just twice, each use costs $5. On the other hand, if you use that $100 personal die cut machine 100 times, the investment pays off.

CLIP COUPONS

Many craft stores offer coupons which allow you to purchase products for up to 50% off. Mark the expiration date of coupons on your calendar and shop before the store promotion expires.

BUY IN BULK

Purchase staples, such as cardstock, in bulk. You will pay less money in the long run. You may also wish to chip in with a group of friends to share the discount and the product.

SHOP OFF THE BEATEN TRACK

Office supply stores, discount warehouses, dollar stores and online auctions often carry scrapbooking supplies at lower prices than specialty stores. Check them out.

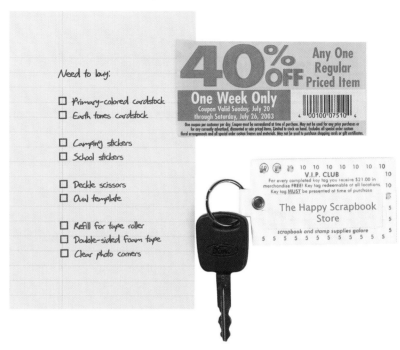

So that you do not clutter your workspace with unnecessary purchases, it is important to practice smart shopping strategies that will help you balance what you want with what you truly need.

PATIENCE IS A VIRTUE

Don't purchase the latest trendy product on a whim. Start a "wish list" and wait to see if the item you want today is the item you still want next week or next month.

BECOME A FREQUENT SHOPPER

Ask if your favorite store has a preferred customer card. You'll save money while indulging your passion for shopping.

Cropping-on-the-Go

Scrapbooking at a friend's house, a crop party, a scrapbooking store or retreat presents even the most organized scrapbooker with unique challenges. Decisions must be made in advance regarding which photos and supplies to take. Oftentimes the impulse is to bring everything just in case you need it (and you most likely won't). A little planning will help lighten your load.

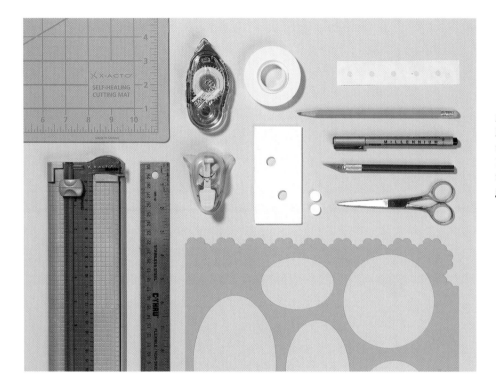

Make a travel cropping kit of basic scrapbooking supplies that you know you will need no matter where or when you crop. This way, even if you receive a last-minute invitation, all you have to do is grab your cropping kit and go!

Getting organized for a crop

Make a travel cropping kit filled with basic scrapbooking supplies that you are sure to need no matter where or when you crop. This will make it possible to "grab and go" even if you receive a last-minute invitation. Include the following:

• Adhesives
• Basic shape template
• Black journaling pen
• Blank scrapbook pages
• Corner rounder punch
• Craft knife
• Metal straightedge ruler
• Page kits (see below and right)
• Page protectors
• Paper trimmer
• Pencil with eraser
• Scissors
• Small assortment of colored cardstock
• Small cutting mat

If you have extra room in your basic cropping kit, you may also consider bringing:

• A couple of pairs of decorative scissors
• Colored pencils, pens or markers

What's a page kit?

When cropping on-the-go, consider bringing along "page kits" in addition to your basic supply kit. A page kit is a packet filled with materials you intend to use to make a specific scrapbook page. For example, a page kit compiled in anticipation of the creation of a child's birthday celebration spread might include party photos, themed patterned paper, birthday page accents or embellishments. It might also include memorabilia such as birthday cards, a napkin or gift wrap samples. If you plan to work on a scrapbook technique—such as stamping, setting eyelets or creating punch art—you will also need to pack the tools and supplies needed to accomplish the task.

The key to making page kits is to do as much planning as possible before leaving home in order to insure a more productive cropping session while away.

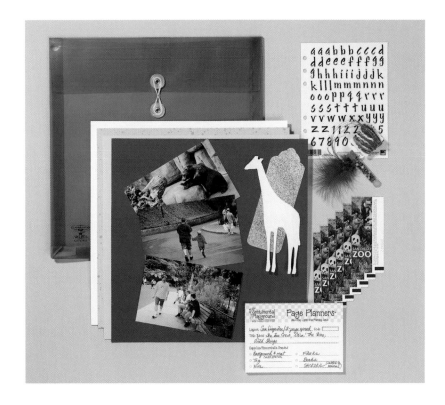

Page kits make for quick and easy cropping-on-the-go. This page kit began with zoo photos. Appropriate background and accent papers, letter stickers, embellishments and memorabilia make the page kit complete. Our page kit is contained in a Generations' Craft Keeper™, which comes in 12 x 12" and 8½ x 11" sizes. Fill out and tuck in The Sentimental Playground's Page Planner™ to keep your page plans on target.

How to make a page kit

DETERMINE CONTAINMENT

Store your page kit in an empty page protector, zippered plastic bag, box, accordion file or other keeper large enough to hold 12 x 12" papers and any page additions. Plan on one "container" for each page kit to keep each photo layout separate and protect the selected supplies. Several companies make products that are perfect for containing individual as well as numerous page kits for cropping-on-the-go.

SELECT PHOTOS

Spread out your pictures. Select high quality photos that truly speak to you. Place one to five photos for each proposed scrapbook page into each page kit container. Toss out or give away photos you don't care for any longer and file away your negatives. Add any correlating memorabilia to the page kit.

CHOOSE PAPERS

Use paper colors that are consistent with the mood, and work well with the hues, in your photos. Choose primary and complementary colors. Select both background and patterned accent papers. Add papers to the page kit and include appropriately-colored paper scraps to use for photo mats or title and journaling blocks.

DECIDE ON PAGE ADDITIONS & COLORANTS

Add pre-made page accents (see pages 76-79) and other embellishments (see pages 63-67) to kits for each layout. Place smaller items like fibers and eyelets in snack-sized zipper baggies before adding them to the larger protectors. If embellishments require special tools, make these beforehand so you don't have to bring the tools themselves. For example, fill a bag with pre-cut punchies so you don't have to transport paper punches. Select and include special colorants (see pages 58-62) that you wish to use on accent your page.

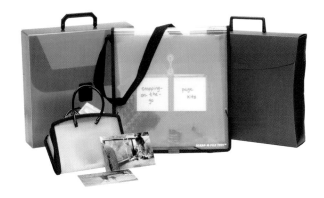

Many manufacturers make totes to contain a number of page kits for easy travel. Try Mochalatte's Super Tote Box, General Box Company's Crop 'N Go™ tote or Caren's Crafts' Scrap-N-File Tote™, to name a few. If you prefer to keep your photos stored outside of the page kits, keep them organized in an accordion-style tote such as Generations' My Generation™ Sassy Scrapper™.

ADD JOURNALING NOTES & PAGE DESIGN INSPIRATION

Place journaling notes (see page 68-70), scratch paper on which you jot down page sketches, potential page titles and journaling ideas into page kits.

INCLUDE TITLE MATERIALS

Include title lettering templates, sticker letters or pre-made titles.

On-The-Go Storage Solutions

If you are an on-the-go scrapbooker, you will need a portable storage unit. While there are many portable storage units on the market specifically designed to hold scrapbooking supplies, general art supply storage products are also useful.

Customized options for the scrapbooker range from backpacks and shoulder bags to cases on wheels and plastic storage totes. Many of these carry-alls have designated compartments and pockets for safely storing tools and supplies—such as punches, stamps, decorative scissors and pens. Many have special compartments for toting 12 x 12" and 8½ x 11" papers and sturdy compartments for storing heavy 12 x 12" albums. Add a luggage identification tag with your contact information for a measure of security, should you and your tote become separated.

Here and on the following pages, we feature a wide array of travel totes for scrapbooking and carrying art supplies. However, companies are continually expanding their product lines to meet the needs of today's scrapbooker, so be sure to check out their Web sites (see our Source Guide) for new offerings.

Immediately after a crop, unpack your travel tote and put tools and supplies away in their storage bins and compartments. Trim paper scraps and file them. Sort and store unused photos and negatives. Add finished pages to scrapbook albums or in a designated "holding container" until you're ready to place them in an album.

Generations' Weekender™ Backpack and Scrappack's Scrappack™

Generations' Memory Tote™, Scrapbook Sally's Paper Packer and Tote, and SCS/Hemline's Sew Easy® Project Bag

Most product manufacturers produce several different types of totes and carry alls for scrapbooking "on-the-go." From backpacks and shoulder bags to handled totes on wheels—you're sure to find exactly what you need to suit your scrapbooking style. Check out the manufacturer web sites (listed in our Source Guide) for each company's latest and greatest offerings.

Generations' Crop Station™ and Plaid's Creative Gear™ Wheel Cart & Craft Tote

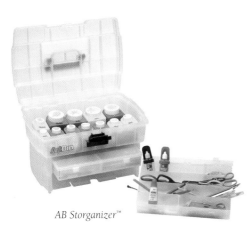

AB Storganizer™

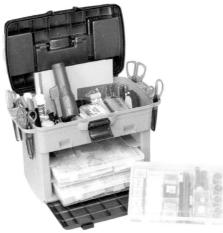

AB Easy View I

AB Quick View™

ArtBin has an extensive line of plastic and canvas totes, tray boxes and carrying cases in an enormous array of styles and sizes. You're sure to find just the size you need for storing your on-the-go tools and supplies—whether it's a little or a lot!

AB Tote 'n Go

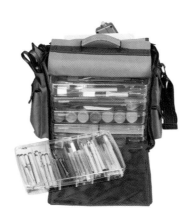

AB Mega Tote

AB Tote Express™

AB Quick Tote

AB Ultimate Solutions Tote™

CIS Paper Taker

Crop In Style, as well as other companies, designs high-quality travel totes and wheeled "pulls" with the scrapbooker in mind. Whether you're looking for a simple backpack, a shoulder tote or a full-fledged suitcase on wheels—even a portable scrapbooking table—there's a lot to choose from! Crop In Style also manufactures a wide array of storage components that fit inside their traveling totes. These storage products can be added to your scrapbooking repertoire over time as your collection grows and your budget allows. Their most recent addition to their growing line: a backpack with wheels, a pulling handle and its own rain poncho (see far below on the right)!

CIS Back Pack

CIS Na Navigator LTD

Crop In Style's XXL

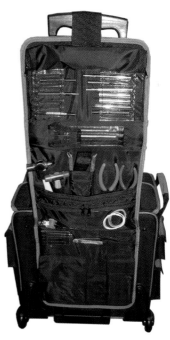

CIS Tool Bag

CIS Na Navigator LTD with Tote Table

CIS Stamp Store

CIS Not Just For Kids Back Pack

Jokari's Scrap'N Stor Carryall™ is a versatile little tote that has a hook for hanging; a shoulder strap for carrying; and an adjustable, rotating stand for desktop or desk-side access while cropping-on-the-go.

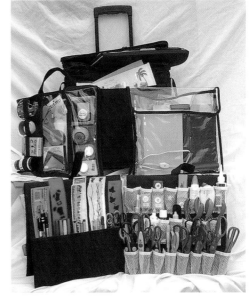

Canvas Collectible's components are sold separately and fit into their square tote in background. Storage elements include Ditty Plus, Protect 'n' Store, Double-Sided Insert and Accessory Insert.

Besides its many smaller totes, Tutto offers Crafts on Wheels™, which you can read more about on page 23.

Crop With This' Paper Express provides ample room for paper on-the-go or to store paper in the workspace.

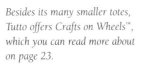

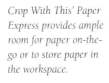

Besides their wide array of plastic paper and sticker totes and cases, Leeco/Cropper Hopper also manufactures a line of on-the-go organizers including The All Terrain Bag (ATB), Scrapbook Tote Bag and the Flat Pack™ Organizer.

Trading Scrapbook Workspaces

Just when you think you "have it all together" in your scrapbook workspace, try "trading" your workspace with a scrapbooking friend to see how your organizational abilities stack up.

The concept is simple. Create a scrapbook page within a set amount of time—such as three hours—in a friend's scrapbook workspace. You may bring with you only one set of photos. Your friend will do the same in your scrapbook workspace. Invariably, the space swap will give you great organizational ideas to incorporate into your workspace once you return home. Try it! This is guaranteed to be among the most fun and educational times you've spent scrapbooking.

The scrapbookers

We found two scrapbookers—Julie Labuszewski and Maureen Behnke—who were willing to take our *Trading Scrapbook Workspaces* challenge. They were instructed not to discuss the theme of their photos or details about their workspaces with each other prior to the swap. Our staff documented the fun, foibles and frustrations the women experienced while visiting each others' homes.

Julie Labuszewski, of Centennial Colorado, invades Maureen's home and personal scrapbook workspace to see just how easily she can create a scrapbook page outside the comfort of her own workspace.

JULIE'S PERSPECTIVE

"I liked the spacious, uncluttered room. Maureen's Memory Garden theme, so beautifully executed, made the space pleasant and inviting. I liked working next to a large window. The natural light, which was gentle on my eyes, illuminated the desktop perfectly. I liked the display of product on the shelves behind me. The colorful selection of glitter, beads and embossing powder inspired me.

"I liked how Maureen utilized and labeled her storage units. There was a storage unit filled with 12 x 12" solid paper, a unit for scrap paper and another storage unit for printed paper. She labeled each smaller folder inside the unit, so finding a specific color of paper was quick and easy.

"I liked seeing labels on the stack of purple interchangeable drawers designed to fit inside a travel tote. I quickly found most of the supplies and tools I needed.

"I liked not having to get out of my chair to get supplies, tools and paper. Everything was conveniently within arm's reach.

"I liked the high-quality office chair. It provided back support and comfort. I won't be attending any more midnight crops where I'm expected to sit in a metal folding chair for three or four hours.

Julie's first stumbling block was trying to find the perfect shade of golden yellow cardstock to pull out the striking color in her photos. There was no match, however.

After selecting a different set of photos to scrapbook, Julie quickly found the paper, tools and supplies she needed to work on a scrapbook page. Having everything within arm's reach made it easy!

As time runs out, Julie's frustration grows as she tries three different black pens to trace over her penciled journaling. The pens were dried out! The fourth pen was a charm and journaling was completed. The last hurdle: no sewing needle or thread to be found for her button embellishments.

"I liked seeing Maureen's work elegantly displayed on the wall in two wooden 12 x 12" frames. I absolutely loved the Sizzix die cut machine. Maureen had a die-cut for every letter of the alphabet. In less than five minutes, I had the headline for my page punched out. I may incorporate this machine into my workspace. Usually, I hand letter all my headlines, which takes time. With three children running around the house, I am going to have to scrapbook faster. A Sizzix machine would be a great solution. It would even give me an opportunity to use up my surplus of patterned paper."

RECOMMENDATIONS FOR CHANGE

Julie's first hurdle: a limited selection of solid-colored papers. "When I showed up at Maureen's house, I brought along some great photos of my son and a thumbnail sketch of the page I had planned on creating. I wanted to find paper to match the striking background color in these photos. I looked though her solid papers but couldn't find the color I needed—a golden yellow. I considered using other colors for the page but I could see they wouldn't work, so I decided not to execute my initial page idea. Fortunately, I had a few photos of my son in the tub. I found a sheet of cobalt blue. Now I was on a roll. In summary, I would have liked a larger selection of colored paper to choose from."

Dried-out pens were another stumbling block for Julie. "When I finished journaling the text on my page in pencil, I looked for a black pen to go over the pencil lines. I found three black pens. Unfortunately, each one had dried-out ink. I was getting frustrated and my time was running out. When I turned around and discovered a complete set of ZIG pens on the shelf behind me, I was ecstatic."

Julie's final impediment included a needle and thread that were nowhere to be found. "I chose to embellish my page with yellow buttons. Usually I sew on buttons. I think this looks more authentic. I wanted to sew on the buttons but I couldn't find a needle and thread. I ended up using sticky dots. Later that day, Maureen showed me where she keeps her needle and thread."

Julie was pretty fond of Maureen's labeling on everything, which made it easy for her to identify and find things quickly. She also liked Maureen's high-quality chair for its great back support and comfort.

Maureen Behnke, of Littleton, Colorado, enters Julie's home with photos in tow to embark on her own adventure of discovery.

MAUREEN'S PERSPECTIVE

"I liked the atmosphere in Julie's office. The café theme invited me to come in and relax and take a moment for myself. Julie even had cappuccino and cookies set up in the entrance hall!

"Another thing I really liked was her 12 x 12" paper rack. The first thing I do when making a page is pick out my background paper. Julie had a tall 12 x 12" paper rack that made selecting just the right color a snap!

"I could tell that organization was a priority in Julie's workspace. She labeled large baskets with all the necessary supplies. For example, she had a basket of adhesives, a basket of cutting tools, a basket of punches, another for stamps and yet another for embellishing tools. Plus, they were all within arm's reach from the work surface."

Playing with Julie's "toys" was to Maureen's liking. "It was fun exploring all of her tools. I used her small alphabet stamp set to make custom tags for my layout. I also enjoyed her selection of punches, which were easy to use with her Power Punch accessory."

Julie's reference materials proved to be handy as well. "I used Memory Makers Quick & Easy Journaling to help me with adjectives to spice up my journaling. Julie even had a thesaurus and a dictionary which came in handy for my page title "Bubbley", which became "Bubbly" in the nick of time!

RECOMMENDATIONS FOR CHANGE

Julie's lighting's got to go! "Julie has a window in her office, but it was an overcast day. The ceiling and small desk lights were not bright enough for detailed work like stamping and embossing. I would invest in an Ott Light or some other craft lighting.

Maureen appreciated Julie's corralling and organization of her supplies, making it easy for her to find just the right adhesives and more.

Julie's café theme was inviting, but Maureen confessed that her lighting "has to go!"

Maureen did not expect her creativity to be affected by trading spaces, but oddly enough, she discovered that her page turned out to be very much like a page Julie would create!

THE AFTERMATH

After trading spaces, Julie and Maureen talked about the experience. "I recommend this to anyone who wants to make significant improvements in their workspace. It forced me to think differently about my workspace. For the first time, I began to think about my workspace objectively—from an outsider's point of view," says Julie. "As a result, I came up with new, creative and more efficient organizational strategies.

"I tossed out my old push-pin bulletin board and purchased a few new magnetic ones. They're the perfect choice because with a magnet you never have to poke a hole in a favorite photo again!

"It was fascinating to hear about Maureen's experience working in my office. For example, since I usually hand letter my headlines, I don't have any lettering templates, lettering stickers or lettering reference books. This drove her crazy! She also couldn't find the blades for my circle cutter. Frankly, I'm still looking for them too. In the end, we found the feedback valuable," adds Julie.

"Oh yeah, the lettering thing," Maureen winces. "Julie is a master at freehand lettering. I, on the other hand, need all the help I can get, thus my Sizzix machine. I had to go beyond my comfort zone and hand letter my title. Sticker letters, which are not my first choice, were in short supply."

And then there's the awkward feeling of working in someone else's kitchen. "This is not something Julie could change, but something built into the experience," says Maureen. "Sometimes I felt like I was an Italian chef working in a Chinese restaurant. The tools were different, the paper was different, even the music was different! Julie and I have different personal styles, which are evident by our offices. I would say Julie's office is more upbeat and chic, whereas I have a more warm, homey office. I did not expect my creativity to be affected by the space I was working in, but my page turned out to be very much like a page Julie would do!"

Both women agree on one thing: "This was a wonderful experience and we would highly recommend it!"

Once past the awkward feeling of working in someone else's workspace, both scrapbookers settled in to complete their task at hand. The ladies met afterward to discuss the day's events. Maureen and Julie are still best scrapbooking buddies and both agree that trading spaces was a wonderful learning experience.

Gallery of Efficient Workspaces

Many scrapbookers have already discovered the joy of scrapbook workspace organization and have reaped the benefits of increased productivity. Let their beautiful workspaces inspire you to begin working on your your own!

Linda Lawrence's (Palm Beach, Florida) husband, Gene, gets all of the credit for designing her highly functional workspace. Besides its sheer spaciousness, the room's other quality traits include lots of closet storage, over-the-door punch pockets on both sides of the door and built-in shelves behind the closet door that are the perfect depth for storing 12 x 12" albums. Linda's quite fond of her sticker and die-cut binders, tilt bins and plastic storage drawers. The self-proclaimed scrapbook addict offers this advice: "Label, label, label," says Linda. "And always be flexible: Out with the old and in with the new!" Way to go, Gene and Linda!

Kathy Gleason's (Crete, Illinois) well-stocked and organized workspace features an astounding array of storage shelving, drawers, slots and racks. Kathy holds monthly crops where guests are amazed how easy it is to find everything—even if it's their first time there! Her best productivity advice? "Label everything so you don't waste time looking for a certain item," says Kathy. "Always put things away after scrapbooking, so you don't waste time cleaning the next time you scrap." We really like Kathy's idea of displaying her die-cut shapes on the wall. Each time she buys a new die, the shape goes up on the wall!

Barbara Gardner (Scottsdale, Arizona) is a professed fanatic about having a place for everything and everything in its place. "My scrap room was designed so most of my supplies are out-of-sight in drawers or on shelves behind doors," says Barbara. Her tidy workspace boasts 40 feet of running countertops, and lots of quality light. "Good lighting is paramount," says Barbara, whose workspace is illuminated by a north-facing window, two skylights, six recessed halogen ceiling lights and under-cabinet lights spaced 2' apart. The 12 x 12" cardstock trays, made by her husband, are "priceless." We adore this room as much as her Persian cat, Jasmine—who sits on the shelf atop the computer and listens to classical music while watching Barbara scrapbook. Very nice!

Linda Owens' (Camarillo, California) 30 square feet of counter space; wire paper racks; custom-made, 300-stamp wall organizer and ample work surfaces dominate the highlights of her efficient workspace. "Excellent lighting is very helpful," says Linda. "And having plenty of work space and a designated place for every item are my best organizational tips." Love that stamp organizer, Linda!

Angie McGoveran (Festus, Missouri) employs side-by-side drawer units beneath an inexpensive countertop for valuable storage space. Pre-fabricated bathroom cabinets and an antique file cabinet round out the storage capacity of her well-organized workspace. Angie used to want an entire room devoted to scrapbooking, but has fallen in love with her shared space at the end of her family room. "I can be a part of what my family is doing while I am scrapbooking," says Angie. Her organizational advice: "Put things away as soon as you bring them home. If things pile up, it becomes a huge job. It's less overwhelming to put stuff away 10-15 minutes at a time." Nice job, Angie!

Kelly Angard's (Highlands Ranch, Colorado) scrapbook workspace features white-laminate modular furniture with plenty of storage shelves and work surfaces. The painted walls (inspired by SEI patterned paper) burst forth with creative energy. We're a bit partial to the wall art, which is fitting for this loyal Memory Makers Books art contributor and writer. Bravo, Kelly!

Additional Resources

If you need even more in-depth help organizing your workspace, there is help available. Whether you like to gain inspiration reading quietly on your favorite sofa or if you prefer to be online with an insightful group of thousands of other scrapbookers, you may find these additional resources useful.

WEB SITES

123 Sort It

Advice and forms to print for organizational use in residential homes and the office.

123sortit.com/toc.phtml

15 Uses For...

interiordec.about.com/library/bl_15uses.htm

Club Mom

Free organization checklists for all areas of the home.

clubmom.com

HGTV Trash To Treasure

hgtv.com/hgtv/trash_to_treasure/0,1792,HGTV_3912,00.html

I Need More Time

ineedmoretime.com

Katie Leckley's Grand Plan for Home Organization Room by Room

members.aol.com/bullseye57/webtest/geto/grandplan.html

Organize Tips

Tips for helping you get organized in your daily life.

organizetips.com

Organized Home

Free advice and printable organizer notebook sheets for home and scrapbooking organization from Cynthia Tower Ewer.

organizedhome.com

Organizing From the Inside Out

Website and book advice from a professional organizer on how to develop an organizational style that suits you.

juliemorgenstern.com

Picture Me Foundation

An organization that gladly accepts surplus scrapbooking tools and supplies.

pictureme.org/newhome.html

Scrapbook Organization Inventory Notebook Worksheets

Free downloadable worksheets from Traditions Matter by Kathleen Aho.

angelfire.com/rock3/tradmatter/scrapbook_inventory_notebook.htm

Scrappers Challenge

An e-mail loop at yahoogroups.com that provides free daily reminders and monthly challenges to help you keep your focus on organizing your scrapbook workspace. Moderated by Kathleen Aho, one of the contributing writers for this book.

groups.yahoo.com/group/ScrappersChallenge/

Sidetracked Home Executives: From Pigpen to Paradise

Pam Young and Sydney Craft Rozen

shesintouch.com/index.html

Sink Reflections

Flylady groups, products and advice for week-by-week home cleanup from Marla Cilley.

flylady.com/index.asp

BOOKS & PUBLICATIONS

Balance Magazine

The magazine about getting and staying organized.

findbalance.com

Clutter's Last Stand by Don Aslett

Good Things for Organizing by Martha Stewart

How to Get Organized When You Don't Have the Time by Stephanie Culp

Improving Productivity By Getting Organized by Joe Peraino, Ph.D.

Is There Life After Housework? by Don Aslett

It's Here . . . Somewhere by Alice Fulton and Pauline Hatch

Lighten Up by Michelle Passoff

Office Clutter Cure by Don Aslett

Organizing Plain and Simple: A Ready Reference Guide With Hundreds of Solutions to Your Everyday Clutter Challenges by Donna Smallin

You Can Find More Time for Yourself Every Day by Stephanie Culp

Additional Credits

Bookplate, Page 3

Scrapbook Workspace of Maureen Behnke, Littleton, Colorado; Photo Christina Dooley

Reader photos

All reader photos appearing in this book were shot with Kodak HD High Definition 400-speed film, made possible by a generous donation from the Eastman Kodak Company of Rochester, New York.

Sources

The following companies manufacture workspace and storage products featured in this book. Please check your local retailers to find these materials, or go to a company's Web site for the latest product. In addition, we have made every attempt to properly credit the items mentioned in this book. We apologize to any company that we have listed incorrectly, and we would appreciate hearing from you.

3M Stationery
(800) 364-3577
3m.com

Accu-Cut®
(800) 288-1670
accucut.com

Akro-Mils
(800) 253-2467
akro-mils.com

Armada Art, Inc.
(800) 435-0601
armadaart.com

ArtBin by Flambeau
(800) 232-3474
ArtBin.com

Artfully Scribed, Inc.
(703) 787-8267
artfullyscribed.com

Artograph, Inc.
(888) 975-9555
artograph.com

Avery Dennison Corporation
(800) 462-8379
avery.com

Beadalon®
(800) 824-9473
beadalon.com

Board Dudes, Inc., The
(800) 521-4332
boarddudes.com

Canvas Collectible's, Inc.
(208) 378-0569
canvascollectibles.com

Caren's Crafts
(805) 520-9635
scrapbooking4fun.com

Charming Ideas, Inc.
(888) 502-8082
charmingideasinc.com

C-Line Products, Inc.
(888) 860-9120
c-lineproducts.com

Collected Memories
Scrapbooks
(866) 483-9391
collectedmemories.com

Collectors Cabinets
(715) 484-5025
Collectors-Cabinets.com

Colorbök™, Inc.
(800) 366-4660
colorbok.com

Crop In Style®
(888) 700-2202
cropinstyle.com

Crop With This
(661) 250-7439
cropwiththis.com

C-Thru® Ruler Company, The
(800) 243-8419
cthruruler.com

Darice®
(800) 894-5990
darice.com

Daylight Company, LLC
(866) 329-5444
daylightcompany.com

Display Dynamics, Inc.
(908) 231-1132
displaydynamics.net

DMC Corporation
(973) 589-0606
dmc.com

DMD, Inc.
(800) 805-9890
dmdind.com

Dymo
(800) 426-7827
dymo.com

Eagle Affiliates
(800) 643-6798
eagleaffiliates.com

Eastman Kodak Corporation
(770) 522-2542
kodak.com

EK Success Ltd.
(800) 524-1349
eksuccess.com

Ellison Craft & Design
(800) 253-2238
ellison.com

Ergonomic Services, Inc.
(303) 904-8333
ergoservices.net

Fiskars, Inc.
(800) 950-0203
fiskars.com

Flex Products
(800) 526-6273
flex-products.com

For Keeps Sake
(801) 967-6664
for-keeps-sake.com

General Box Company
(912) 283-5716
generalbox.com

Generations®
(800) 905-1888
GenerationsNow.com

Handango™
handango.com

Highsmith®, Inc.
(800) 558-3899
highsmith.com

Hunt Corporation
(800) 283-1707
hunt-corp.com

Inventor's Studio, The
(866) 799-3653
inventorsstudio.com

Jokari/US, Inc.
(800) 669-1718
jokari.com

Jotters
(877) 568-8371
jotters.net

K & Company
(888) 244-2083
kandcompany.com

Kokuyo U.S.A., Inc.
(877) 465-6589
kokuyo-usa.com

Leeco Industries, Inc.
(800) 826-8806
leecoindustries.com

Lifetime® Products, Inc.
(800) 225-3865
lifetime.com

Light Impressions®
(800) 828-6216
lightimpressionsdirect.com

LNS Software Solutions, LLC
(253) 850-2457
LNS-software.com

Magic Scraps™
(972) 385.1838
magicscraps.com

Making Memories
(800) 286-5263
makingmemories.com

McGill Inc.
(800) 982-9884
mcgill.com

Media Group/Sewing Genie™
(203) 406-1000
SewingGenie.com

Mochalatte™
(866) 344-0129
mochalatte.com

Novelcrafts
(514) 582-3208
novelcrafts.com

Ott-Lite® Technology
(800) 842-8848
ott-lite.com

Pageframe Designs
(877) 55-frame
scrapbookframe.com

Paintier Products, LLC
(586) 822-7874
paintier.com

Pampered Chef®, The
(800) 266-5562
pamperedchef.com

Pencil Grip, Inc., The
(888) 736-4747
thepencilgrip.com

Photographic Solutions, Inc.
(800) 637-3212
photographicsolutions.com

Pioneer Photo Albums, Inc.®
(800) 637-3212
pioneerphotoalbums.com

Plaid Enterprises, Inc.
(800)842-4197
plaidonline.com

PrintFile, Inc.
(407) 886-3100
printfile.com

Provo Craft®
(888) 577-3545
provocraft.com

Quantum Storage Systems
(305) 687-0405
quantumstorage.com

QuicKutz, Inc.
(888) 702-1146
quickutz.com

Rubbermaid
(888) 895-2110
rubbermaid.com

Scrap Kings
(408) 782-9798
scrapptopia.com

Scrapbook Sally
(866) SB-SALLY
scrapbooksally.com

ScrapNCube
(800) 216-4992
scrapncube.com

Scrappack
(866) 228-1458
scrappack.com

SCS USA/Hemline
(800) 547-8025

Sentimental Playground, The
(207) 655-7109
sentimentalplayground.com

Sizzix®
(866) 742-4447
www.sizzix.com

Stamppadcaddy.com
stamppadcaddy.com

Stampin' Up!®
(800) 782-6787
stampinup.com

Sterilite Corporation
sterilite.com

Sturdi-Craft, Inc.
(800) 888-3905
sturdicraft.com

TidyCrafts
(800) 245-6752
tidycrafts.com

Traffic Works, Inc.
(323) 582-0616
trafficworksinc.com

Tutto®/Mascot Metropolitan,
Inc.
(800) 949-1288
tutto.com

Twin Ray
(323) 939-9059
twinray.com

un-du Products, Inc.
(972) 279-6633
un-du.com

Uniek, Inc.
(800) 248-6435
uniekinc.com

Verilux, Inc., "The Healthy
Lighting Company"
(800) 786-6850
healthylight.com

Westex Corporation
(908) 624-0093

Westwater Enterprises
(201) 935-6220
westwat.com

Xyron, Inc.
(800) 793-3523
www.xyron.com

Sources II

The following companies donated products used to decorate boxes featured in this book. Check your local retailers to find these products, or go to a company's Web site for the latest information.

American Traditional™ Stencils
(800) 448-6656
americantraditional.com

Clearsnap Inc.
(888) 448-4862
clearsnap.com

Delta Technical Coatings, Inc.
(800) 423-4135
deltacrafts.com

Design Originals
(800) 877-7820
d-originals.com

Hot Off The Press, Inc.
(800) 227-9595
CraftPizzaz.com

Plaid Enterprises, Inc.
(800) 842-4197
plaidonline.com

Wallies®
(800) 255-2762
wallies.com

Sources III

The following companies manufacture scrapbook supplies that were used to stock the storage containers featured in this book. Please check your local retailers to find these supplies, or go to a company's Web site for the latest product.

Page 34
Label maker (Dymo), Pens (American Crafts, EK Success, Sakura), Post-It® notes (3M), labels and dividers (Avery), adhesive (Hermafix), punches (Hyglo, McGill).

Page 35
Stamps (EK Success), punch (Hyglo), pens (EK Success).

Page 38
Acrylic paints (Delta), Mod Podge® (Plaid), transfer (American Traditional).

Page 39
Film border punch and square punch (Family Treasures), Film (Kodak).

Page 43
Patterned paper (Design Originals), letter stickers (EK Success), Mod Podge® (Plaid).

Page 44
Acrylic paint (Delta), Mod Podge® (Plaid), stamps (Hero Arts,Inkadinkado, Plaid, PSX Design, Stampabilities, A Stamp in the Hand, Stampin' Up!), ink (Clearsnap, Tsukineko), stickers (Karen Foster Design), ribbon (Garden Gate Designs), stencil (American Traditional), fibers (Rubba Dub Dub).

Page 48
Crimpers (Fiskars), brayers (source unknown).

Page 49
Cutters (Carl, Fiskars, Lion, Puzzle Mates, Shaping Memories, X-acto).

Page 51
Scissors (Armada Arts, Family Treasures, Fiskars, Provo Craft), punches (All Night Media, Carl, EK Success, Emagination Crafts, Family Treasures, Hyglo/American Pin, The Punch Bunch).

Page 52-53
Stamps (Club Scrap, Design Originals, EK Success, Hampton Art Stamps, Hero Arts, Limited Edition, Magenta, PSX Design, Rubber Stampede, Stampin' Up!), Unmounted Stamps (Design Originals, Lost Coast Design, Oxford Impressions, Wordsworth), Mod Podge® (Plaid), floral napkins (Plaid), acrylic paint (Delta).

Page 53
Templates, stencils, and decorative rulers (C-Thru Ruler, Dream Weaver Stencils, Lasting Impressions, Scrap Pagerz).

Page 56
Adhesives (3L, 3M/Scotch, American Tombow, Art Accents, Duncan, EK Success, Glue Dots, Paper Mate, Pioneer, Ranger, Suze Weinberg, Therm O Web, US Art Quest); adhesive application machine (Xyron).

Page 57
Wallpaper cut outs (Wallies), stickers (Stickopotamus).

Page 59
Paints (Angelwing Enterprises, Chartpak, Delta, Duncan Enterprises, Ranger Industries, Sakura Hobby Craft), applicators (EK Success, Loew-Cornell, Tsukineko).

Page 60
Embossing powders (Ranger, Tsukineko, Suze Weinberg), embossing pens (Tsukineko) pencils (Chartpak, Staedtler).

Page 61
Pens and markers (EK Success, Sakura, Staedtler), stamps (Clearsnap, Hero Arts), ink (Clearsnap, Stampin' Up!), organics (Hot Off The Press).

Page 62
Chalk (Craf-T Products, EK Success), metallic rub-ons (Craf-T Products), applicators (Craf-T, EK Success, Tsukineko), ink pads (Clearsnap, Hero Arts, Ranger, Tsukineko), Dauber Duos (Tsukineko).

Page 63
Metallics (Artistic Wire, Biblical Impressions, Eyelet Co., Global Solutions, Halcraft, Making Memories, Provo Craft, Rubba Dub Dub, Scrap Yard 329).

Page 64
Shaved ice and tinsel (Magic Scraps), buttons (Blumenthal Lansing), tiny glass marbles (Halcraft, Magic Scraps), sequins and confetti (Westrim), beads (Bead Heaven, Blue Moon Beads, JewelCraft).

Page 65
Fibers (On The Surface, Rubba Dub Dub, Scrapbook Sally); floss (DMC).

Page 66
Sewing Genie™ and threads (Media Group, Inc.), ribbons (Offray).

Page 67
Organics (All Night Media, Colorbök, Hot Off The Press, Magic Scraps, Rubba Dub Dub, U.S. Shell), Clay (Provo Craft, Sculpey by Polyform Products).

Page 68
Binders and books (Memory Makers).

Page 70
Acrylic paint (Delta), letter stickers (PSX Design), Mod Podge® (Plaid), patterned paper (Provo Craft).

Page 72-74
Cardstock (Bazzill, DMD), patterned papers (Design Originals, Hot Off The Press, Karen Foster Design, PSX Design).

Page 73
Mod Podge® (Plaid), clip art (Dover Publications), ink (Clearsnap), patterned paper (Design Originals, Karen Foster Design, Magenta), stickers (EK Success, Club Scrap), acrylic paints (Delta), paper accents (EK Success), colored pencils (Prismacolor), stamps (A Stamp in the Hand), label holders (Anima Designs), ribbon (Offray), and hemp string (Pulsar).

Page 76
Pre-made page additions (Colorbök, Deluxe Cuts, Design Originals, DMD, EK Success, Ever After, K & Company, JewelCraft, Westrim Crafts).

Page 78
Stickers (EK Success, Me & My BIG Ideas, Mrs. Grossman's Paper Company).

Page 94
Cutting mat, paper trimmer and X-acto knife (Hunt Corporation); templates and ruler (C-Thru Ruler); scissors (Mrs. Grossman's Paper Company), vellum adhesive (3M), corner punch (EK Success), tape runner (American Tombow), foam dots (Ranger), glue dots (Glue Dots International).

Page 95
Stickers (Stickopotamus), wire (Artistic Wire).

Index